# Finding Faith in the Field

# Finding Faith in the Field

Benjamin Duane Hylden

*Jesus Loves you :)*

*Benjamin Hylden*

*Psalms 23*

Published by Retelling
www.Retelling.net

Produced by Samizdat Creative
www.samizdatcreative.com

Cover design by Cynthia Young
www.youngdesign.biz

Cover photos by Larry Biri + PhotoLyric/iStock

print ISBN: 978-1-938633-59-1

# Contents

*But when the kindness and love of God our Savior appeared, he saved us, not because of righteous things we had done, but because of his mercy. He saved us through the washing of rebirth and renewal by the Holy Spirit, whom he poured out on us generously through Jesus Christ our Savior, so that, having been justified by his grace, we might become heirs having the hope of eternal life.*

Titus 3:4-7(NIV)

# Foreword

When we went to pick up two of our children at Bible camp, my husband and I were excited to see them again, since they had been away a week. I knew the car ride home would be full of stories packed with potentially life-long memories. One of the first things my son Andrew said to me was, "Mom, you have to meet my camp counselor, Ben. You have to hear his story."

I invited Ben onto my radio program, and he was more than willing to share. I have interviewed several people with amazing stories about their lives and faith. Ben's story stuck out to me as one that would help restore people's hope in Christ.

Before Ben's accident, his walk of faith could have represented the journey of any number of people, with their doubts and struggles. But the journey he's been on since then shows the truth that there is a God, and that He has a plan to strengthen us.

Throughout his story, Ben captures the emotions many people feel, and glimpses of what we will see and feel in the future. While reading this book I kept thinking about the song, "I Can Only Imagine" by Mercy Me, as I pictured the experiences Ben shares in this book.

Ben's story reaffirms my belief that, whether given a moment in a field with God, experiencing a story someone has shared with us, or having a moment of clarity ourselves, we are all on a journey, and we're here to help each other. His story helps us realize that we can make a difference, and that through God all things are possible—especially when we're willing to share the love of Christ with others.

I'm thankful to my son Andrew for making sure I heard Ben's story. If you have ever wondered if Heaven is a real place, or wondered why you are here, I'm grateful you are about to read through Ben's journey of faith from the field through the road to recovery.

Missy Ohe
Christian Speaker and Radio Host

# Jesus, Take The Wheel

*Our God is a God who saves; from the Sovereign LORD comes escape from death.*

Psalm 68:20 (NIV)

## Good Friday, April 6, 2007

April 6, 2007, Good Friday, started out as a normal spring day. A sophomore at Park River High School, I woke up early to finish all my chores on the farm a mile from our house. At noon I headed back home to change clothes and get ready for my physical therapy appointment to treat an injury I'd sustained playing basketball. Even though I didn't have much time, I decided to take a few extra minutes to try on my suit coat to make sure it fit well for our upcoming prom. As I passed the farm on my way into Park River, my sister was still there. She had always reminded me to wear my seatbelt, but she told me later that she regretted forgetting to remind me that day. But I never listened to her anyway.

Since I was running late, I took an old back road that I used to make up time, usually when I was late for school, which was often. It was the quickest way into town since I could go as fast as I wanted. The weather was pretty cold that day, which is normal for North Dakota in early April, so the roads were half frozen over with ice. I decided to slow down a little from my usual 70-75 miles per hour to only 60 mph.

I drove an old Buick Le Sabre that tended to accelerate even when I wasn't pressing on the gas. As I was driving by the pasture where we keep our cattle in the summer, the car accelerated and I started to swerve. I tried to regain control, but I couldn't steer the car on the ice. I was now in panic mode; I didn't know what to do. I hadn't slowed down because I expected to manage the spin; consequently I flew 60 miles per hour into an approach.

As I hit, my head slammed against the steering wheel, deploying the air bag. When it popped open, all of the gunpowder inside it burned my left forearm. The gearshift stabbed into my right leg, and the windshield caved in on me. I was terrified; it all happened so fast.

I wasn't wearing my seatbelt, of course, so as my car flipped several times I flew out of the passenger door head first into the half frozen field, slamming the left side of my face into the ground.

Not knowing where I was, I lay there in extreme pain, feeling like I'd been hit by a train. My entire body hurt. My face felt like it was crushed from the inside out. I had bitten through my tongue, so I was constantly swallowing blood as I lay there on my back. My leg felt like it had been stabbed all the way through. In a few moments my eyes and face swelled up so badly I couldn't see any more. I was alone and there was no one to help me.

Or so I thought.

The only thing I could think of was to try to reach home. I couldn't walk, so I started crawling on my back. I wasn't sure if I was even going in the right direction, but I didn't care. Unfortunately I couldn't do it; the pain was too much to bear. I wanted to scream, but I couldn't because the roof of my mouth was broken in half.

Suddenly someone grabbed me and said, "Sir, please lay down." Then I heard another voice talk to the first person. I had no idea who these people were. I called them the "two nice people" in my mind.

They tried to calm me down and convince me to lie still, but the pain was too much. Everything hurt; it felt like a bomb had exploded inside of me. The people were saying things to me, but I could only faintly hear because my ears were filled with dirt. I could barely breathe.

Everything went into slow motion. I was still constantly swallowing blood, so it made it even harder to breathe because my lungs were filling up with my own lifeblood. I knew my life was about over. I didn't think I could take much more. There was not enough air and too much pain. I never in my wildest dreams thought my life would end like this.

The two nice people both held me still so that I would not sustain further injuries, but that couldn't stop the fact that I knew I was going to die. As I lay there, I lost all hope and just thought about my family and friends and wished that they were with me, so I could say goodbye and tell them that I love them.

At a point, there was no air left, so I took what I thought would be my last breath.


Meanwhile, my parents had a couple of errands in Park River that day. It was Good Friday, and my mom wanted to buy Easter candy to hide for my brother Andrew, who still liked to hunt for it. My dad had arranged to meet for lunch with a family friend who rents a field from us.

They took off soon after I did.

It seems as if Jesus was driving that day because my dad says he does not know to this day why he turned down that road, since he normally took the main road into town. But he did, and they came upon a car in a field owned by my dad's cousin, Mark Hylden. It was so smashed up and covered with mud that it looked like it was burned, and at first my dad thought kids had been up to some prank, so they kept driving. However, as he drove a little farther, out of the corner of his eye he saw something black move out in the muddy field.

"Lana, there's someone out there," he said to my mom. He pulled over and they both hurried out of the truck to see.

They were shocked to find a teenage boy full of blood and mud, and on the verge of death. The boy was beaten up so badly that they couldn't tell who he was. They never suspected it was their son; they thought I was already in town.

The boy was struggling to move, so they held him and my dad said, "Sir, you need to calm down. We're going to call an ambulance. Everything will be all right."

Dad went back to the pickup to call 911. My mom ran over to grab a coat that had been thrown from the car in order to cover the boy, because it was so cold.

Mom says as soon as she felt that coat, she knew it was my dad's, the one that had been on the backseat of my car. With a foreboding, she glanced around the icy field, and saw other debris that belonged to us. She said she put the coat over the boy, but couldn't tell it was me because my face was swollen like a balloon. But when she looked down at my feet, with the shoes ripped off, there were my long, skinny feet.

When Dad came back she said, "Kenny, this is our son," and they both started crying and praying.

When my body went limp and I quit breathing, my dad said, "Ben, you gotta wake up!" He slapped my head back and forth to try to revive me, like he would do to a new-born calf who wasn't breathing, to get him going.

While I was lying in the field, before I stopped breathing, I had no particular thoughts about death. But what I experienced during those silent minutes changed my perspective on death forever.

I came back and kept fighting to breathe. I could faintly hear sirens in the background. They put me on a stretcher and placed me in the ambulance very carefully. At first they considered taking me to our local hospital in Park River, but the paramedics said I would never make it if we went there because my injuries were too severe. They decided to take me straight to Altru Hospital in Grand Forks. My parents were told I had very little chance of surviving the trip there, but that was the only choice they had.

My folks in the pickup couldn't keep up to the ambulance. She was going 90-100 miles an hour. But the EMTs said I only had a few minutes to live. Later that day, the lady who drove the ambulance told my parents, "I broke the speed limit the whole way, even though it was breaking the law, because I knew I had to get him there quickly or he would not have made it."

Many miracles happened on that day for my life to be saved. "Everything had to work together for him," in order to keep me alive, my dad said afterward—like the EMTs deciding to take me to Grand Forks instead of Park River. It is ironic that my dad's meeting with the friend who rented our field would be rescheduled three times to that day at that very time. There is also no reason that my parents should have taken that road, and especially on that day when my dad had already decided to take a different route. Yet the greatest miracle on that day remained a secret, even from me, until much later.

# Little Did I Know

*Immediately Jesus reached out his hand and caught him.
"You of little faith," he said, "why did you doubt?"*

Matthew 14:31(NIV)

While growing up, I was raised in a Christian home by two loving parents, Kenny and Lana Hylden. I have one brother, Andrew, who was 11 at the time of my accident and one sister, Christine, who was 18. Our parents taught us about Christianity, strong life morals, and the importance of hard work.

We lived ten miles southwest of Park River, North Dakota, on a dairy farm, so from a young age I learned what hard work was all about. Our farm was not big by today's standards, but with only my family to take care of 250 head of cattle, 80 milk cows, and 600 farmland acres of wheat, barley, corn, potatoes and pinto beans, it was definitely a big operation. The tough demands of dairy farming include no days off. Regardless of the weather, even in a blizzard or tornado, the cows still have to be milked twice a day, 365 days a year. However, the farm has been in my family for 125 years, so it is very important to my family and a huge part of our heritage.

My parents both have strong Christian values and

taught us children the importance of them. Since my parents needed to take care of the farm every Sunday, they would send us to Sunday school and church with our grandpa, who lived on the family farm and helped raise us. But my parents were always there for me.

When we were young, they sent us to the Park River Bible Camp, hoping that our faith would grow in Jesus Christ. Going to camp was always my favorite week of the year, but not for the right reasons. I loved camp because of the waterslide, to hang out with friends, and to meet new girls.

At a young age, I believed that Jesus was our Savior only because of my parent's biblical teaching, but He was not an important part of my life and my faith would have been compared to that of a mustard seed, very small. Little did I know how that faith would someday miraculously grow and blossom through the power of God's love.

Some nights, I would lie in bed and pray, not because I had faith God would answer, but because my parents said praying was good. Even though I was always polite and had good manners, looking back now I was a very selfish kid, considering I would usually pray for myself even though I didn't have the faith that God would answer the prayers anyway.

As a kid, I mostly focused on sports. I always figured I would one day make millions in the NBA. Most of the time, that was all I thought about. I started playing basketball at the age of six during Park Board, a youth basketball camp in Park River. I instantly fell in love with basketball and was asked to play on an all-season team with some of my friends. Our team's success made me believe we were better than everybody else and that someday, when we were all in high school, our team would win a high school basketball State Championship.

Starting in 7th grade, a lot of things changed for me. I started playing junior high football, along with basketball, and the idea of someday winning a State Championship in both sports became my number one focus. That was where my heart was.

Also, peer pressure started to kick in. Many of the things my parents had warned me about started happening, like being asked to drink, smoke, and party. Although I did not give in to the peer pressure, it was still a very tough time in my life. Many of my close friends chose a different path than I did, so we stopped hanging out and our close relationships ended. I wanted to start drinking so I could stay close to my friends and fit in, but I could never forget what my parents had taught me and let them down. Even so, I started to lose interest in my family because I always wanted to be playing sports, working out, and hanging out with my friends. And working on the farm made me moody, changing me from the happy kid that I used to be.

I became angry with my parents whenever I had to work, whether it was milking, feeding the cows or giving them straw. It irritated me when my dad made me come home after school during harvest time to help on the farm rather than allowing me to stay to lift weights every day. Usually I kept my anger inside, but one night after school I was so mad I blew up and started yelling at my dad outside of the barn. My parents were sad to see the person I was becoming, and that I was growing away from them and God. The happy, life loving boy I once was, was gone. Depression was a reality.

Sadly, I caused a lot of hardship for my family, and it dampened the tight knit relationship we used to have when I was younger. The worst part, though, was that it made me mad at God for everything that I did not like in my life.

When my freshman year started, it felt like a whole new world. Going from the top of junior high to the bottom of high school was a big change. Most of the time, I thought about high school sports, because we had all waited for them since we were young. Personally, I could not wait for basketball to start, so I could play my favorite sport and get off the farm.

Before the basketball season started, an unexpected tragedy set my faith back even further. On the night of September 8, 2005, around 11:00 p.m., my sister came running into my bedroom crying uncontrollably. I was sleeping, and I woke up shocked to see her in tears. I tried to ask her what was wrong, but she couldn't speak.

Finally, after asking her over and over again why she was crying, she told me, "Grandpa died."

The words shook me, and I didn't want to believe it was true. There was no way that was possible. I had just been talking to him two hours earlier and he seemed to be fine.

My family drove over to the farm where he lived, and when I saw an ambulance and the paramedics, my heart completely sank, knowing that he was actually gone. At first, I couldn't cry because it was all too shocking, and I didn't want to accept it, because I could not imagine my life without him.

Ever since Christine, Andrew, and I were kids, he had been there every day helping my mom and dad raise us. When my parents couldn't take us places because they were working on the farm, he was there and willing. Not many grandparents would often go out of their way to take their grandchildren first to the local gas station to get them something to drink, next to the Dairy Queen to buy them a blizzard, and finally to Hot Stuff to buy them some pizza, just to see them smile and make their day. Well, that was my grandpa.

There usually was not a day that went by that I did not see or talk to him, watch a Minnesota Twins game with him, or go with him somewhere. He was the first person who taught me about the game of basketball and how to shoot a basketball, which meant a lot to me.

Grandpa's death was very hard for me to get over. I wondered why God would take him out of our lives. It felt like it was not his time yet, because he was still very healthy for his age and had never given any signs that death was near. His unexpected death, and confusion as to why, distanced me further from God and filled my heart with sadness and anger.

During the basketball season I experienced another unexpected setback, a back injury that sidelined me halfway through the season only fueled the bitterness that I was already feeling towards God.

My relationship with my family also continued to suffer due to my decreasing interest in farming. Many nights I wouldn't talk to my parents at all, just because I was angry about having to work.

Things were getting worse instead of better, as I got older. My grades started to suffer because of my obsession with sports. My parents tried talking to me about my grades and attitude, but it was to no avail. My bad attitude towards my parents and God had not changed.

Even though my attitude was horrible, I still did not give in to peer pressure in high school. Mostly for the reason of getting kicked out of sports if I was caught, and because there was a part of me that did not want to let down my parents. Even though I was mad at them, I still loved them.

My basketball dream started to come true during my sophomore year. I began starting on varsity along with three other classmates, Ryne Anderson, Jay Jelinek, and Max Otto. We ended the year in 4th place in the playoffs, so I thought we would be unstoppable our junior year and make our first run for a state title.

Our early success really went to my head. I started to become arrogant and thought I was untouchable. And even though I had been doing well in basketball, I gave God none of the credit for it. My relationship with my family continued to suffer and it was only getting worse while I grew arrogant and self-centered, with God nowhere in sight.

However, on one normal day in the spring of my sophomore year, my life would be changed forever.

# Death Upon Me

*"If you believe, you will receive whatever you ask for in prayer."*

Matthew 21:22 (NIV)

In the ambulance, my lungs struggled to keep up on 100 percent oxygen. The medics worked on me the whole way, keeping me alive as we rushed to the hospital. The emergency room doctors and nurses were shocked to see a sixteen-year-old in critical condition, all bloody and full of mud. They were not sure how long I would be able to stay alive, so they quickly had to assess my injuries to determine the extent of the damage.

I had bruised my lungs, kidneys, pancreas, liver, and small intestines; had crushed an artery in my right leg; had broken my pallet in half; had broken my nose in nine places; had badly bruised my right hip; had broken four ribs; had severed my tongue; and had shattered most of the bones in my face and my brain was bruised and bleeding. My parents asked the doctors how bad my face really was, and they said to take a potato chip and crush it; that's what my face looked like. At first, they thought I had lost all of my teeth because when I had broken my pallet, all of my teeth had been pushed up into my nasal cavity. But a few days later my teeth dropped down.

Even though it was very hard for the doctors, they had to tell my parents that their son probably would not make it. Even if I did somehow survive, they would most likely have to amputate my right leg, since it had not been getting blood for the last few hours.

They also said that since my organs were damaged so badly, they would most likely have to remove parts of them as well. The injuries to my head would be fixed later on, depending on if I lived or not. The news was very hard for my family to take, but they ultimately just hoped that I would somehow survive.

First, the medical team needed to put a new blood vessel in my leg, so the blood could travel throughout my entire leg. They had to act quickly and the surgery needed to go perfect, so they did not have to amputate. Thankfully, the surgery went amazing, and they were able to save my leg. Next, expecting to remove parts of my organs, the surgeons opened me up for exploratory surgery to see the extent of the damage. My liver and lungs were the most damaged, but to their surprise, my organs were not damaged to the point where they had to remove anything.

Unfortunately, as they were stapling me shut, they forgot to make sure all the air was sucked out from around my lungs. Instantly, my lungs collapsed, and I stopped breathing.

The doctors tried everything, but nothing was working to get me breathing again. Eight people were trying to save my life. The head surgeon came out to the waiting room and told my parents that if they couldn't get me breathing again in the next five minutes, they could come say goodbye to me.

It broke my parents' hearts to hear that, but they did not give up hope. By that time, twenty-some friends and family were in the waiting room with my parents. One of my relatives, after hearing the bad news, stood up and led the room in prayer that God would yet again save me and keep me alive.

At the time, no one knew how God was already answering that prayer, nor the miraculous sight I was seeing.

While my family and friends were all praying, the doctors located a lung specialist in the hospital. Right away, he told them to insert chest tubes to remove the air from around my lungs. Then they opened up my throat and put in a trachea.

Miraculously, I came back after not breathing for several minutes. Everyone was overjoyed to hear the good news that I was still alive. My family and friends did not give up the hope that I would get stronger and survive this tragedy. They kept praying for me and believed that I would make it.

"Great, so he's all right?" my father asked the doctor when he came to the waiting room and explained what had happened.

"No, I am sorry, but he most likely won't make it through the night," the doctor replied, because my lungs had not yet started swelling from the beating they had gone through. It would be nothing less than a miracle for me to survive the next three days, because the doctors told my parents that my lungs would most likely start to swell up and shut down. A nurse later told my parents that I had no more than a five percent chance of making it through the night, because of the critical condition I was in. Although, he didn't use the word "miracle" with my dad, the doctor told him that the only things that were working in my favor at that point were that I was physically fit and a non-smoker—and prayer.

As the sun came up Saturday morning, I was still alive and my lungs had not swelled up at all. My mom and dad came in to check on me every ten minutes just to make sure I was still breathing. Although it saddened them to see me in the hospital so beaten up and bruised, they were both very happy that I was still alive and fighting when I should not have been. My mom told me that she prayed for me all day every day and truly believed that God was keeping me alive by answering her prayers as well as the prayers of many others.

However, while my mom and many others stayed streadfast in prayer for my survival, my dad wanted to, but decided to stay silent. My dad was wholeheartedly a Christian man and has based his way of life upon the Bible as long I have known him, but his faith in prayer was lacking. He said he knew he should have prayed and wanted to, but he feared that he would have hated and never forgiven God if he had prayed but I still died and was taken away from him.

As Saturday proceeded, I stayed stable. The doctors would not let anyone in to see me other than my family because they were afraid it might upset me, even though I had been put in an induced coma, so I could not hurt myself while moving. Nothing really changed; they just hoped and prayed I would make it.

While my parents remained with me at the hospital, my dad's friends told him not to worry about the farm. He heard the next morning that there were eighteen people in the yard to help milk the cows and tend to the farm work.

## *Easter Sunday, April 8, 2007*

As Easter Sunday arrived, I was making real positive steps forward. My little brother Andrew came in to see me that day. It was very hard for him to look at my disfigured body and face, so he had to leave the room. To cheer him up the nurses had an Easter egg hunt for him in the waiting room.

My mom and dad slept in the waiting room every night just in case something happened, since the doctors now predicted that I would die in one of the first three days following the collapse of my lungs during surgery. They figured my body was too weak and had been through too much to keep going. To their surprise, my body began to rapidly heal.

I had gone from being a few moments away from death, to doing some of my own breathing. I was now taking 13 of 20 breaths by myself, compared to breathing solely by machine. The doctors were shocked with my progress and said that I was doing much better than expected. Even with the positive steps, my survival was in God's hands.

# Saved But Scarred

*So do not fear, for I am with you; do not be dismayed, for
I am your God. I will strengthen you and help you; I will
uphold you with my righteous right hand.*

Isaiah 41:10 (NIV)

*MONDAY, APRIL 9, 2007*

On Monday, they performed tests (EKG, CAT scan, ul-
trasound, MRI) to see how my heart and brain were doing. Other than the severe concussion I sustained, the test
results came back completely normal. The swelling and
bleeding had stopped in my brain and my heart was doing well.

I was doing so well that they had taken me off life support, but had to put me back on after my tests, because the
tests took so much energy out of me. My breathing kept
getting better, considering that while I was still on a venti-
lator, I was only doing about 50 percent of the work. Due
to how serious my injuries were, the doctors estimated
that I could be in the ICU for up to three weeks, possibly
longer, recovering.

With my dad at the hospital most of the time, someone
had to take charge of the farm and make sure everything
ran smoothly. For the first week while my dad stayed at

the hospital, my little brother Andrew and my cousin, Josh Hylden, who were familiar with the herd and the farm, oversaw all of the chores. Andrew had always loved farming, but he never dreamed that he would have to run the farm when he was only eleven years old. He said that the day of my accident was the day he became a man. He had to keep his feelings together, go to school, run the farm, and not break down.

Some years later, he told my dad that it was the toughest time of his life, because he wanted to be at the hospital too. I'm very proud of him and always will be for stepping up at such a young age and leading the farm when it needed him the most.

Many friends and family continued to come from all over to help with the farm. Dad said that at one point there were so many people, some we didn't even know from neighboring communities, waiting to help at our farm that he had to turn people away because there were no jobs left. People would come by, but there would be so many vehicles there already that they would just keep driving. He was very grateful for all the help, because when he was at the hospital, he then did not have to worry so much about the farm.

At the time, my sister was a freshman at the University of North Dakota. On the day of my accident, there was no one at the farm to help my cousin, Josh, take care of the farm, since everyone was at the hospital with me. Knowing the circumstances, she graciously went home with her good friend, Tami Daley, to tend to the farm because my parents knew the farm would be in good hands with her there. It broke her heart to leave me at the hospital, but she is very strong person, so my parents knew they could rely on her. However, after help came to the farm, she came to see me every day since she was only a few minutes' drive from Altru Hospital. She helped my mom and dad with whatever they needed, and she also kept everyone updated on how I was doing through CaringBridge on the internet. It was very hard for her to keep going to school, update my progress and not break down, but she stayed strong.

In the meantime, my mom continued to pray day and night for my survival, while staying with me at the hospital the whole time.

---

"As I walked into Altru Hospital, I immediately saw Ben's dad, Kenny. Usually happy and joking around, Kenny was much different this time with a sad and serious look on his face. He told me that Ben was in severe condition and that there was a good chance that he would not make it. However, he did tell me that I was able to go in and see Ben, so that was a bright spot; but at the same time it was scary because I did not know what to expect. As I walked into Ben's room in the ICU, I was completely shocked to see the endless cords going into his body, but most of all, how distorted his face had become from the accident. I did not want to believe that what I was looking at was my best friend, but I had to accept that this was the reality. As I then walked closer to him, I was overwhelmed with emotion and began to cry uncontrollably. I felt like it was not fair for something this horrific to happen to a guy like him, and that it was not his time yet. As I continued to cry, I began begging God to heal him and keep him with us."

-Ian Myrdal

## Tuesday, April 10, 2007

On Tuesday, I made even more positive steps forward. It was the first time, since going into my coma that I was beginning to slightly respond to anyone. Early Tuesday afternoon, I held my mom's hand along with her holding mine. My mom would sit in the hospital every day since my accident and pray that I would respond to her. When I held her hand, it made her very happy because she knew her son was back, and it gave her hope for the future.

At that point, things were looking very well for me. I was breathing on my own for three to four hours on that day, so that was the best news yet. The doctors were now convinced that I had made it and escaped death, for my body was healing at an incredible rate, which was considered truly a miracle.

The doctors warned my parents, though, that even with me coming out of this alive, I may be a very different person when I wake up. Due to my brain injuries, there was a good chance that I may have to relearn how to do a lot of normal everyday things like reading, writing, walking, and talking. They predicted that if I did go back to school, I would have trouble learning and would need assistance. Also, the chance of my playing sports again was very low due to my brain and physical injuries. It was hard for my parents to hear, but they were just happy that I was alive.

## Wednesday, April 11, 2007

On Wednesday I started to come out of my coma. I opened my eyes, and I didn't know where I was or what was going on. The first thing I remember was three men trying to hold me down to put in my feeding tube that I kept pulling out. I was scared, so I fought for dear life, and even punched one of them.

They brought my mom in to settle me down. In fact, they had to call her in many times because she could work with me like nobody else could. She would put her hand on my hand and say, "Ben, you have to do this. Let them do it." And I would calm down.

Sometimes the pain made me violent, but they couldn't sedate me enough because I was too close to death. Fortunately, they said it was good I still had a fighting spirit.

Shortly after, I began to respond with nodding and hand gestures. When my little brother Andrew told me that he wouldn't be back for a couple days he asked me to squeeze his hand and I was more than willing, because I didn't want him to leave. My family and the doctors were very happy with that because it was the first loving emotion I had demonstrated, since waking up.

### THURSDAY, APRIL 12, 2007

I was moved up to room 302 on Thursday. At first, the doctors had estimated that I would be in the ICU for several weeks at least, but I was only in there for five days. They removed my chest tubes since my lungs were working much better, but I still had some trouble, so they kept a trachea in my throat to help me breathe.

As the days passed, I became stronger and more alert to my surroundings. I began feeling all the pain and how uncomfortable everything was. I pulled out my feeding tube every chance I got, so they decided to let me try to eat liquid food rather than inserting a feeding tube into my side, which would have been very painful. Thankfully, I adjusted to the liquid food, but, even without the feeding tube life in the hospital was hard to deal with. Life in room 302 was plain miserable.

As I became fully awake, I began to question where I was and why I was there. I was shocked to hear that I had been in a car accident and had stopped breathing twice. My mom and dad told me the whole story, and that it was they who had found me in the field. The "two nice people" had been my parents.

The more my parents and I thought about how everything turned out and how it all happened, the more it was clear that God had saved me, for reasons I didn't know at the time, for reasons I'd been mysteriously told but didn't yet remember.

After realizing what God had done for me and giving thanks, I had to face my long recovery and all the pain that came with it. I remember waking up thinking normally, but not being able to do the normal things that I took for granted. I was used to being active every day and playing sports, but now all I could do was lie in bed and heal.

After a few days of being in room 302, I was totally conscious and out of my coma, so the doctors decided to tell me what my injuries were, my limitations, and my long-term plan. It was devastating to hear about all my injuries and what I couldn't do. They told me that I may be in the hospital for months recovering. I may have minor brain damage, so it would affect me greatly in school. But worst of all, there was a good chance that I would never be able to play sports again.

It was hard to take, but there was something inside of me that kept telling me not to give up. I believed with all my heart that I would play basketball next season, even though the doctors considered that impossible.

I had become extremely weak from not moving for weeks, and couldn't even attempt to walk because of the surgery on my leg. I was seeing double vision because of the trauma on my brain. I could not talk because of the tracheotomy in my throat, which produced a hole and my voice could not get through anymore, so I could only communicate through writing. I could not eat because the bones in my face were shattered, so it was impossible to chew and all I could eat were Jello and protein shakes.

It was distressing to wake up with extreme pain, double vision and not being able to walk, talk, or eat. Many times I became so uncomfortable and miserable that I would start to sweat, shake, and panic, because I wanted so badly to just be normal again.

However, even though it was a very tough time, my friends and family kept me motivated, and I looked forward to returning home to see everybody. While in the hospital I had many visitors, some who came every day. It meant the world to me to see my friends and family while recovering, because they were a part of what kept me going every day, to keep fighting and not give up.

While in the hospital and out, I was amazed by the overwhelming support, love, and prayers my family and I received from my class, the Town of Park River, friends from Bible camp, and the surrounding area. There is a sign at the edge of Park River that reads, "A town with a heart." Now my family and I believe that is an understatement after all the love and care we received in the midst of my accident.

My high school class from Park River was one of my biggest supporters. Many of them came to see me frequently in the hospital or sent me words of hope and encouragement. They also set up a successful spaghetti feed benefit to help my family with all the expenses involved with my accident. It was amazing to think about all the work they did to help me and my family.

One of the stories that will forever stay with me was about a guy in my class named Cody Boyle and his sister, Misty. They were both in Grand Forks when they heard I'd been in an accident, and they instantly dropped what they were doing and rushed to the hospital. They could not see me, so my parents told them what had happened.

Besides my parents, who had followed the ambulance to Grand Forks, they were the first ones to show up at the hospital. When my parents told me this story, it meant a lot to me because even though I was not close friends with Cody or Misty, they still cared enough to rush to the hospital to see how I was. This story is a prime example of the love and support my family and I received from my classmates.

My parents showed me all the messages I received on the CaringBridge site, and the countless cards, texts, and e-mails. They gave me hope. To this day, I have not forgotten the people and the words they said, and never will.

I can't say enough about my mom and what she did for me during those days. She is a relentless praying woman. When I was in the ICU, she pretty much lived in the waiting room, so she could come check on me all day to make sure I was doing okay. When I moved up to room 302, she still never left me. She would sleep on a wooden bench in my room at night and sit right by me holding my hand during the day. My mom was my rock and I never wanted her to leave. Without her there with me every day, I do not think I would have been able to stay sane.

My first goal was to be able to walk, because the doctors said I could not go home until I could walk down the hallway and up and down the stairs. They said it would take me weeks to be able to walk, but I was walking down the hall just days after they told me that.

After a week of being in room 302, it was time to perform surgery on my face to fix all the broken bones. I was very scared and nervous thinking about the surgery. I remember writing to the doctors, "Make sure I don't die" as they were wheeling me into the elevator. They reconnected all the bones in my face with wires, sewed my pallet back together and fixed my nose as well as they could, so I consider the surgery a success.

After a few days following facial surgery, I was focused on one thing, and that was getting home. My motivation had increased and so had my strength. I finally was able to start walking alone, and was happy to walk to the bathroom for the first time, knowing that I was walking by myself and not so helpless anymore. However, my happiness quickly turned to sadness when I looked in the mirror.

The person I saw was not the same person that I knew before my accident. It felt like I was looking at myself in a nightmare. As I stood there looking at that brown-haired, six-foot-tall person, my green eyes overflowed with tears. I now realized just how distorted my face had become, with all the swelling, multiple cuts, bumps and bruises that covered it, and my nose being broken, crooked. I tried to soften the image that I was seeing and to think positive by smiling and being happy in the fact that I was walking by myself. But as I smiled, I quickly noticed the large gap between my two front teeth caused by the roof of my mouth being broken in half. I felt like I did not know the face that I was looking at anymore and helpless because there was nothing I could do about it.

My body had dramatically changed as well. As I examined my body, I realized that I had lost every muscle I had worked so hard for before my accident, and every ounce of fat seemed to be gone. My body looked severely frail and weak from losing forty pounds in only two weeks. I was a skeleton.

It was a very hard moment to take, knowing how much my body had changed and what my face had become. As soon as I walked out of the bathroom, though, that motivation kicked in again, and I asked the nurse for dumbbells to start lifting weights in bed. I could only lift five pounders at first, but I figured that was better than nothing. Every time I lifted, I had the thought of next basketball season in the back of my mind.

As the days progressed, so did I. I was becoming stronger every day and I was doing everything the doctors wanted me to do. Every morning the doctors came in and checked on me, and every morning I asked them if I could go home. So far, they would always say, "Not yet" but I knew one day they would have to say, "Yes" because there would be no reason for me to be in there anymore. However, even with the progression and optimistic outlook, they continued to doubt whether I was able or strong enough to survive outside the hospital.

# Chasing A Dream

*Jesus replied, "What is impossible with men is possible with God."*

Luke 18:27 (NIV)

## MAY 2007

I entered the hospital on April 6, 2007, with little chance of survival and left the hospital on April 23, 2007, able to walk, talk, and think normally. I had been in the hospital for seventeen days instead of the projected months. I healed much faster than expected, which everyone considered to be a miracle. I didn't know it yet, but a miraculous spiritual journey was still ahead of me.

Leaving the hospital that day was one of the most amazing moments of my life. Breathing fresh air, walking on green grass, and feeling the wind are all things I had taken for granted, but they became things that I grew to cherish. I have now learned to always appreciate the little things, because you never know when they may be taken away from you.

It seemed I'd been away for years. I missed everything about home, even the farm. I wasn't a big fan of the farm, but I missed it more than I ever thought possible. It seemed incredible to walk around the barnyard, seeing the baby calves in their pens and all the cows in the barn, because there were times in the hospital I thought I may never see the farm again.

It was much nicer waking up the next morning in my own bed in my own house, but reality kicked in when I realized I was still in the same situation as the day before, but just in a different environment. I struggled with the post-surgery pain in my abdomen, face and leg, no longer having the luxury of pressing a button for pain medication, and the medication I had now was nowhere near as strong as the medication in the hospital. I couldn't walk yet without someone to protect me if I fell, so that meant I had to rely on my mom or dad at all times. In fact, I needed someone to stay with me constantly, in case something went wrong and I needed help, so my mom decided to leave her teaching job to stay at home with me.

For the next month, my days would consist of waking up, watching television, and continually walking longer each day from one side of our house to the other. It was tough sitting in the same chair all day watching television, because I was such an active kid before my accident. My mom literally did everything for me because I was dependent like a baby.

Once the hole in my throat from my trachea healed, I began talking again and proved that my speech was not affected at all. However, I still could not see clearly. The doctor suggested we find a dairy farm to provide nutrient-rich whole milk straight from the cows. The pure, whole milk would help my brain heal quickly, so I could hopefully regain my normal vision, the doctor said. To his surprise, we told him we knew just the place, considering we owned one. After one week of being home and drinking our dairy cows' milk, my vision returned to normal.

Since the bones in my face were still healing, I couldn't chew food yet. I also had numerous stitches in my mouth, so I had to be careful no pieces of food got stuck in them. The only foods I could eat were mashed potatoes, yogurt, pudding, Jello, spaghetti, and eggs my mom and dad prepared for me. Eating the same food every day grew old fast, plus I really wanted to start eating more so I could regain the weight I had lost in the hospital.

As the days went on, I started to become negative about everything. Some nights I would sit in bed and cry because of my distorted face and the massive amount of weight I had lost. It was tough to see how small and frail I was. I also missed playing basketball and hanging with my friends, two of the most important things in my life.

I simply missed being a normal kid, and I started to feel sorry for myself. On one hand, I knew God had saved my life and I was very thankful for that. But on the other, I wondered why this happened to me and why He saved me. Many people would tell me that God had big plans for me, and somehow, deep down I felt that was true, but at the moment, it was hard for me to believe.

However, I had people in my life who wouldn't let me stay negative. My dad would come into my room every morning to see how I was doing and keep motivating me to not give up. My mom did the same thing all day as we were at home together.

One of the biggest motivating factors that kept me going was a note left by my high school basketball coach, Mr. Scherr. It said that he expected me to be back the next season as his starting forward. I read that note often to give myself hope. Every doctor told me that it was impossible for me to make it back to play next season. There was nothing I wanted more than to prove them wrong, and that there is no such thing as impossible. Life was very tough, but I never once doubted that I would someday be normal again.

At this point I could barely walk and I ran out of energy quickly. But even though I was weak, I still really wanted to

*Note from Coach Scherr.*

go to school to see my friends. About three days after I came home, I went in to see everyone. The feeling of love from everybody was overwhelming; it was amazing to think about what they had all done for me and my family. I was planning on eating lunch with my classmates, so I brought in puddings and Jello, but to my surprise, they were having spaghetti so I could eat it with them. It was an awesome feeling being able to eat lunch with all of my friends again, but it was hard for me to leave them and go back home.

Life soon became very lonely out on the farm. Al-

Dear everybody,
thank you
all very much for the support verbally and spiritually
It has meant a lot to hear all the good things
s said. That is what has kept me going. And I just want
to say thanks to the ones who prayed and ones
who came here to see me. It was a delightful surprise
and I truly believe it has been a miracle. I made it.
I was beat up pretty bad. But I'm making it. So just that
to all and I can't wait to see all of you

Ben amin !

Hylden

*Thank you note from Ben.*

though my mom was with me, it still could not make up
for the loss and emptiness I felt not seeing my friends every
day. However, several friends of mine including Amanda
Barclay, Emily Mondry, and Chelsey Lutovsky, and a hand-
ful of the guys from my class would come visit me regularly to brighten my days and help me get to the next. Another friend, Breanna Novak, had began working on our farm
while I was in the hospital and came to see me after work
each day, which was also a huge uplift.

Although I was bored at home most of the time, I still
stayed busy each morning going into Park River with my
mom or dad for my physical therapy, a requirement for getting out of the hospital early. My physical trainer, Joe, was
a genuine guy and a great trainer. He motivated me every
time I went in there to keep fighting and not to give up,
no matter how hard it was or how much it hurt. He knew

how badly I wanted to play basketball next year, so he kept me focused on that. Anytime I was about to give up because it was too hard, he reminded me about my dreams of playing again. The only way I was going to play again was if I first learned how to walk properly and pushed myself. I knew he was right, so I pushed myself to the limit every day to get stronger, faster, and mentally tough.

Walking normally again was much harder, and more of a mental challenge, than I anticipated. I was dragging my feet since I was so weak, but as I got stronger Joe pushed me to walk like I had pride again. I needed to walk normally before I could pass physical training and move on to the next step in achieving my dream. He gave me exercises to do at home every day to strengthen my legs and arms. At first, I did them, but after a few days I became physically and mentally drained, and I already wanted to give up.

My mom, however, would not let me. She is a very loving woman, but a very tough woman at the same time. Every time I would doubt myself and say I couldn't do something, she would come right back and say that I could, but I had to believe in myself first. She was not going to let me give up no matter what excuses I tried making. She made me do all of Joe's exercises and would watch me do them every day to make sure I didn't cheat. She and I also went on walks every day to improve my endurance.

During that time, my mom taught me to always work hard even if no one is looking, because it builds character and it will take you to places in life that seemed impossible.

After a month of being home, I was walking normally, lifting small weights, and walking farther than I ever dreamed possible a month before. Also, as I became stronger and as my double vision went away, I started doing the homework that I had missed while I was in the hospital. I was expected to miss all of next year's school year, so for me to already be doing homework seemed remarkable.

With all the things I had to be thankful for, I still found myself down a lot about life and the situation I was in. It was very hard accepting what my life was, because before my accident my whole life was sports, and at the moment that was something that was impossible for me to do. My dad would come talk to me every time he was not in the field and motivate me to not give up, remind me of all the positive things that came out of my accident, and most of all that I was still alive when I should not have been. Our long talks helped me stay focused each day about my dream and what I wanted to accomplish—to come back the following year and play basketball again.

In six months, I would have to gain back a majority of the forty pounds I had lost, go from not being able to walk to sprinting up and down the court, gain back some of my muscle, regain my reflexes and coordination, and most important of all put all those things together on the basketball court to work in rhythm again. I knew it was going to be a daunting task, but I was up for the challenge. It was all worth it to play basketball again. Plus, I wanted to prove every doubter and person wrong who said or thought I could not do it.

## June 2007

As June came and I had been home for a month, the bones in my face had healed, so I could start eating harder food and more variety. It was awesome being able to eat foods that I had not been able to eat in over two months, but the most important thing to me was that I was able to eat meat again, so I could start putting back on muscle and weight.

At first, my appetite was small from not being able to eat anything but soft foods, but that quickly changed. At one point, I was eating twelve scrambled eggs mixed with hamburger and bacon along with two glasses of milk at each sitting. My dad would make me these meals every morning when he was done with the field work, and my mom would make me spaghetti every afternoon to give me the energy I needed to get through each day.

I wasn't expected to be able to do push-ups or lift serious weights until August, but I started all of it mid-June. I did not need to do my physical training exercises anymore since I was well past them by now. It was crazy to think how far I had come since only a month earlier when I could barely lift a five-pound weight, let alone a glass of water. This motivated me to keep working harder every day. The next task at hand was to get my legs back in shape.

Getting my legs back in basketball form was going to be a long, painful process, especially for my injured right leg. I continued to walk with my mom a little farther every day. I would measure how far I walked each time by the posts along the road marking one of our pastures by our house. I would try to at least walk to the next post every time I walked. There were good days and bad days, but if I was ever having a bad day to where I thought I was too tired to keep walking, my mom would hold my hand and reassure me that I could, that I just had to push myself past the limit.

She always reminded me on our walks how blessed I was to be alive and how thankful she was to still have me. She also made sure I knew that no matter how tough life would get that God would always be there to help me, just like He was on the day of my accident. However, He had done more for me than save my life that day, but she didn't know that and I didn't remember yet.

What she was telling me about God always being there for me really started to sink in, and I truly started to believe it. I began talking to God on my own all day and my relationship with Him began to strengthen.

On one of my walks to our mailbox and back to our house, which was about a fourth of a mile, I noticed my legs started to feel normal and strong again. I didn't try to run because I was scared I might overdo it, or hurt myself, which would set back my progess. However, that was all about to change.

One day, I was talking to my Uncle Joel and Dad on the farm when I had an overwhelming urge to run. I did not know where this urge or strength came from, but I was shocked to suddenly have it. In the middle of our conversation, I told my dad I had to go and I started running home. My dad yelled at me to stop, so I wouldn't hurt myself, but I kept going. While I was running, I didn't know how I was doing it, because it was not supposed to be possible at this point. It was exhilarating being able to run like that again, especially since it reminded me of running on the basketball court. Most of all, it fueled my ultimate hope that I would return for next year's basketball season.

After that half-mile run home, I truly felt normal again for the first time since the day of my accident. I also had a feeling that I had never felt before. It was a feeling of true joy that I realized came from being close to God. It was a feeling that I never wanted to go away, but I knew at that moment that my mom was right. God is with you wherever you are, whether it's while you are running or alone in a frozen field.

I also started to realize that the urge and strength to

run did not come from myself. It came from God. He made it possible for me to run when it was supposed to be impossible. I began starting to lean on God with my life and recovery because I now knew that anything was possible with Him and that He would always be with me no matter where I was or what I was doing.

"Have I not commanded you? Be strong and courageous. Do not be terrified; do not be discouraged, for the Lord your God will be with you wherever you go" (Joshua 1:9 NIV).

## JULY 2007

After I ran for the first time, my confidence soared and my recovery accelerated greatly. By mid-July, I was running, doing push-ups and sit-ups, and shooting around on our basketball hoop outside every day. Even though I could not play in a real basketball game, it felt amazing being able to work on my shot again and get back into the rhythm of dribbling and shooting.

Just a month earlier, I was only able to do fifteen push-ups at a time and walk a fourth of a mile, but now I was able to do at least fifty and run a mile. I was getting closer to my dream.

At that point, I was back working on the farm again. Even though I had never enjoyed the farm work, it felt good being back working with my family. While I worked, I always found ways to keep running and lifting. I volunteered to do physical labor, since I wasn't able to get into the weight room. I carried pails of water, spread bales of straw, or helped my dad in the shop; everything helped. When I wasn't doing farm work, I ran sprints to one end of the barn and back. I knew every sprint helped, even if I only had time for two or three. I would also bring a basketball with me to the farm, so when I had a chance on break, I would practice my dribbling.

Some days, the work really wore me down, but I knew the only way I would be able to come back next year was if I pushed myself past the limit every day. I also knew that God was with me, and more than anything else, He motivated me to keep going.

Along with my growing physical strength, I started to see other areas of my life get better. Since my body was stronger and my endurance was higher, I was able to go more places with my friends and not be so exhausted when I came back. I still could not drive, but I was blessed to have good friends who would pick me up, so I could go with them.

I was especially thankful I could once again walk up and down stairs. At the beginning of the summer, I had to crawl up and down the stairs at my friends' houses because my legs were not strong enough to hold me up. Watching me scramble up and down the stairs always gave my friends a good laugh, but that phase in my recovery was finally over, thank goodness.

My relationship with my family greatly improved during my recovery as well. Before the accident, I was always mad at my parents for making me work on the farm when I would rather be playing sports, working out, or hanging out with my friends. I never realized how hard they both worked to give me the life I had, nor did I realize how nice of a life I did have—like having two parents who love me and each other, a brother and sister who love me, and being given everything I needed in life plus much more.

Looking back on crawling in that cold, frozen field, and remembering the sadness I felt thinking that I was going to die without saying goodbye to my family and telling them I loved them for the last time breaks my heart, knowing the way I treated them before my accident. It makes me realize what is truly important in life.

I wasn't especially close to my little brother before my accident. I didn't give him much attention because I always had other things going on that seemed more important. That all changed after my accident.

I'd only seen Andrew a few times while in the hospital because he was in school and working on the farm, and didn't have time to come see me. I was so happy to be with him again that for the first week I made him sleep in my room on the top bunk.

I shiver when I think what could have happened if Andrew had been with me in the car. Usually Andrew rode in to school with me, and most days I would take the same road I took the day of my accident because it was faster than taking the highway. I always drove fast, never thinking I might have an accident.

I am forever thankful Andrew was not with me that day, because he could have been killed. I'm not sure what I would do without him. This experience has made me appreciate and love him more than he will ever know. It also has brought us as close as two brothers can possibly be.

As summer progressed, I was afraid my low endurance level would prevent me from attending Park River Bible Camp, the place where I had my favorite childhood memories and had met some of my best friends. As much as I loved the annual camp and seeing my friends, I was afraid I might try to do more than I was capable of and hurt myself. My parents were scared of the same thing, because they knew how excited I get at camp, and how badly I want to do the things I used to do. However, we made plans for me to pace myself and the camp made accommodations so I could rest whenever I needed to.

Starting out at camp, I was excited to see my friends and to be able to leave my house for a week. But as the week progressed, my excitement quickly turned into exhaustion. I wanted to keep up and do everything that my friends were doing, but my body was not strong enough yet, and I was simply not ready for that level of activity for that length of a time. Many times during the day I would have to go back to the cabin to lie down for a while, even though I would have rather been out with my friends having fun. During the day, the camp had three hours of various activities, or we would go to Icelandic Park to swim and play games. At night, we played large group games like Outpost, or they took us to the Park River pool to swim. I tried my best to keep up with my friends during all the activities, but I realized it was just too soon for me. My mind told me to keep going, but my body would not let me.

It made me sad that I couldn't keep up with my friends, since we had so much fun other years. I'd been going to camp every year with Tyler Lindell, Evan Horter, and Cole Mapes since we met at a winter retreat in fifth grade and have made some of my favorite memories there with them. We were known as trouble makers, but at the same time to make camp fun for ourselves and others. However, thinking back on all the memories only made things worse.

One afternoon, while all my friends were either playing four square or basketball, I went off by myself and sat by a tree. My friend Haylie Holmgren came up and asked me what was wrong. At first, I didn't want to talk and just wanted to be left alone, but she persistently tried to find out what was wrong, and I finally gave in. I told her that life was not fair because of all the negative things resulting from my accident three months ago, and how much my life had changed because of it. At camp, we talked about God every day and how great He was and how much He loved us. But I wondered how a God who is supposedly that great and who loves us that much would let something this devastating happen to me. I didn't understand His plan for me, and all I could do was keep feeling sorry for myself.

At first, I expected Haylie to feel bad for me and console me. But she did the opposite, which I never saw coming. Almost in tears, she told me that I needed to quit feeling sorry for myself and be happy for all of the positive things that came out of my accident. She expressed how blessed I was to even be breathing, considering how many miracles had to happen in order for my life to be saved. And my life had changed for the better, since I had become closer to my family and, most importantly, to God.

Haylie is one of my dearest friends whom I had met at summer camp in our elementary years. My parents told me that on the day of my accident, while many of my friends and family were in the waiting room praying that I would pull through and escape death, a young girl they did not recognize walked into the waiting room alone. The girl was crying and seemed to be very scared and lost. Since my parents did not know who she was, they asked her what her name was and who she had come to see. She answered, "Haylie," and she had come to see me. As I became stronger and was moved up to room 302, Haylie visited me often, and was overjoyed that I was doing better, but most of all that I was still alive.

While talking to me by that tree, she was trying to get

me to realize that even though there were things that were negative after my accident, the fact that I was still alive outweighed all of the negatives combined and that I should feel blessed by God, not betrayed. Even though it was a short talk, it was very impactful. At first, I didn't take what she told me to heart, but after thinking about it for the rest of that day and night, I realized she was one hundred percent right. I needed to be thankful for all of the blessings in my life, and most of all for the second chance of life that was given to me.

As camp came to a close, they showed some inspiring videos to help strengthen our faith. As I watched, I started to tear up and those few tears quickly turned into many. It was the first time, since my accident that I cried because of happiness and thankfulness rather than sadness. I became overwhelmed with joy, because even though I did not ask for it nor did I deserve it, I was graciously granted the greatest gift any person could ask for—life.

For my birthday that summer, several people helped me celebrate the fact that I was alive. The moms of my teammates on my off-season basketball team threw me a surprise birthday party and picnic at Homme Dam near Park River. It really meant a lot to me, because it showed how much they cared about me and how happy they were that I was still alive.

After camp that year, I had a whole new outlook on life. I started thinking that I was actually blessed to be in the accident, because it made me into a stronger person and helped me appreciate every second that I was alive, since you never know what second may be your last.

As the summer progressed, so did I. I kept getting stronger mentally and physically. I worked mostly on my homework every day that I missed during my time in the hospital. Teaching myself the material was the hardest part, and some days I became very tired. Throughout the summer, it was a struggle to get it done, but my mom kept me focused and reminded me that even though I loved basketball, school would take me much farther than sports ever would. Keeping that in mind, I slowly but surely finished all the work I was supposed to do before the summer was over. I was also running and lifting weights every day. Things were looking good for me to achieve my goal and dream—to play basketball again, but I was unsure if I would be able to adjust to the new lifestyle of going to school every day.

# The Good, The Bad, The Ugly

*"I have told you these things, so that in me you may have peace. In this world you will have trouble. But take heart! I have overcome the world."*

John 16:33 (NIV)

## FALL 2007

On the first day of school in August, I was excited to go back to be with all my friends for my junior year, but at the same time, I was nervous because I didn't know how my body would react to the new tasks of an entire school day. I was also nervous because driving into school that day was the first time I had driven without my mom, dad, or sister with me since the day of the accident. As I was leaving home that day, I made sure my little brother and I wore our seatbelts. My dad made sure I knew that taking the old back road was now off limits even if I was late, so I took the highway in to town from then on. It was a special moment for me driving Andrew into school that day, just knowing that he was next to me in the vehicle and still alive.

As I arrived at school, I was given a very warm welcome from all of the students and teachers. I was back in the real world with all of my friends and I felt normal again.

I met with my principal, Mr. David Beckman, before

school started and told him my worries about my ability to last through the entire day. He reassured me that if I ever became too tired to remain in class that I could rest in the teacher's lounge, which made me feel better knowing that my principal was willing to work with me and my possible limitations.

It felt good to sit in a desk again, surrounded by my friends. I had missed this so much in the hospital. Once again, it was one of the little things that I had taken for granted in my life. It actually made me appreciate school and all of the positives that were involved in it, which five months ago did not seem so positive.

That day I was waiting for my body to become tired, but it never happened. At lunch, I could eat anything, since all of the bones had healed in my face. In the afternoon, I expected my body to surely become tired, and that I would have to lie down. My parents and I had figured I would be overwhelmed for at least the first week because of the new environment, the change of pace, and the mental stress of school again. Instead, I made it through the whole day with energy to spare. I went home that day on a high of happiness and energy, but as soon as I got home, I fell onto my bed and slept until my mom woke me up for school the next day.

At the beginning of the school year, classes took so much out of me I had no energy left for working out. I was not mentally or physically ready yet to play football, but I knew basketball season was coming up quickly, and I had to work my hardest every day to be physically and mentally ready to play. With increased endurance and strength, I gradually began to lift weights for a limited amount of time after school. My parents worried that I would over-do myself, so I had to be home at a certain time every day.

I was very intense about my workouts; I had to be ready in three months. Even though I could run and sprint short distances, I knew that I had to do much more than that when it came to playing basketball. I had to have the coordination to dribble, pass, and shoot the ball while running up and down the court as fast as I could.

I needed the overall body endurance to keep doing the high speed pace for a whole game, and I needed the strength and explosion in my legs to drive past defenders, jump above defenders for rebounds, and defend opponents everywhere on the floor. I also needed the mental strength to focus during the game to put all of my physical attributes together. So even though I was months ahead of schedule, I still had a long way to go before I could actually play basketball again.

Each day in the weight room, I started out by using the elliptical for half an hour. I knew I should start out slow and work my way up, but I was too impatient and wanted to play basketball too much. Instead of starting out on a low level on the elliptical, I put it on the highest and began the workout. The pain was almost unbearable, but I just tried to ignore it. I also pushed myself while lifting weights. I would go as long as I could until I couldn't move anymore or until I had to go home. Joe, my physical trainer, had told me that when I began working out again, the pain would be almost unbearable to the point I would cry and I would think I couldn't keep going, but in reality, I could. My body could keep going if I became mentally strong and pushed through the pain.

Every day after working out, I went to Cenex, the local gas station, and bought a blueberry muffin, a bag of jerky, and four quarts of chocolate milk. I did this to replenish my body with the nutrients I needed through the milk, to put on weight through the muffin, and take in extra grams of protein through the beef jerky. After I had eaten all of that, I would head home and eat again.

After working out with the intensity that I did every day, I needed to eat as much as I could to put back on the weight I lost during my workout as well as the weight I lost in the hospital. I was still very skinny and frail, but I continued to work each day to put on weight and muscle.

The doctors had warned my parents that there was a good chance I would be mentally deficient, or would need a lot of help in school due to the major injury to my brain. To make it easier for me, my teachers had lessened the amount of homework I'd missed, and I managed to finish it during the summer. But now, I had to do the same work in the same timely manner as everyone else, so this was the real test for me.

At first, the school insisted that I receive extra help and time on my homework, but I immediately declined because I wanted to be the person I was before my accident, and I had come too far physically to doubt my mental capabilities. Many people thought I was expecting too much of myself too soon, and that it would take time for my brain to heal and my mental strength to come back. Actually, their doubts about my limitations and abilities fueled me to prove them wrong. I refused to listen to the doubters and insisted on all of the normal classes, with no extra help.

When the year started, it was difficult adjusting to the amount of work and to paying attention in class for so long. However, as the weeks continued, I began to readjust to the normal school life, earning even better grades than I had been getting before the accident. I even made the A honor roll for the very first time, which overjoyed me. I had defied the odds once again and proved to everyone, including myself, that I was the same person as before my accident, but even more driven to succeed.

## Winter 2008

Basketball season started soon, and with it came intense practices with our assistant coach, Mr. Omdahl, running us each day. Mr. Omdahl had been my eighth grade math teacher and my assistant basketball coach since my freshman year, but he was more than just my coach and teacher. I looked at him as a role model by how he treated others and lived his life. He was always there for me, and I could always talk to him. The doctors told me after I came out of my coma that one of the main reasons I survived was because my lungs were so strong. If Mr. Omdahl hadn't run me so hard during my sophomore basketball season, I may not be alive right now.

During my first practice back, I realized the transition back may be harder than I thought. I had been working on my shooting, dribbling, and post moves, but I hadn't played in any real games yet because I didn't want to risk the chance of injury before the real season started. I had only regained twenty of the forty pounds I had lost. A lighter body is a positive for running, but definitely a negative as a post player in basketball.

Before my accident, I had always been the bruiser down low who was usually bigger and stronger than most opponents. Now, it was harder for me to post up, play post defense, and box out against the other posts who were much bigger and stronger than I was. I had to adjust by using my speed and shooting as advantage over my opponents.

I thought my dream of starting in our first game that

season would actually be coming true. My coach, Mr. Scherr, told me that physically I looked good, and that he was very impressed with how I was playing. As he named the starters for our first game, I expected my name to be called, but to my surprise, it was not.

I felt sad, mad, and confused. I had worked for months to come back as a starter, and I felt like a complete failure. I was mad at Mr. Scherr because I felt I had earned the right to start. But mostly I was mad at God for giving me false hope, only to let me down after all the work I had put in. And I was confused because I didn't understand why God had motivated me this whole way and helped me to do the impossible, only to fail in the end. To me, it didn't make sense that He would do all these things for me for nothing.

When I got home that night, my parents saw I was not my usual happy self, and they knew right away that something was wrong. I told them what had happened, and they had a much more positive approach than I did about the situation. They tried to tell me that I was not a failure, considering everything I had accomplished and overcome after my accident. But I couldn't help feeling like a failure, because I hadn't achieved my goal.

They also tried to tell me not to be mad at Mr. Scherr or God, because they were just looking out for me. And even though I felt like I was ready to start and play, maybe I really wasn't yet. They encouraged me to consider that even though I had not reached my own goal of starting the first game of the season, I had reached God's goal for me, because He wouldn't bring me through all that for nothing.

He had a bigger and better plan for me, but I just had to be patient. I would soon learn more about His plan than even my parents thought.

All summer I'd imagined myself running out to the

court for the starting lineup, but that would not be the case tonight. Sitting on the bench while they announced my friends' names was definitely not easy. I kept hoping my coach would surprise me and have them call my name, but the game started without me.

Midway through the first quarter, Mr. Scherr looked down the bench and told me to check in. Many thoughts ran through my head as I jumped up and headed to the court for my first game since the accident, like my doctor telling me I could not possibly play basketball this year, and all the work I had put in to get to this point. I was back playing basketball, the game I loved, with Justin Mozinski, Ryne Anderson, Jay Jelinek, and Max Otto—my classmates, teammates, and most of all, friends that I loved.

I had a hard time adjusting to the real game speed and the physicality down low. It was instinct for me to play tough down low, but I just was not big or strong enough anymore. I came to the frustrating realization that I was not the same player I used to be, that I was not ready to start after all, but I still did the best I could. I had come too far to give up.

After the game, I learned Mr. Scherr had actually wanted me to start, but he couldn't get the image of me in the ICU out of his head and he was afraid I might get hurt. I understood and appreciated his concern for me, but at the same time, I did not want him to be scared of playing me.

As the season continued, my skills developed game by game. I finally started in the fifth game of the season. Running out for starting lineup was a moment I will never forget; I had finally accomplished my goal. It was the ultimate satisfying feeling, and it felt as if a huge weight was lifted off my shoulders. Our team was doing extremely well, and I was slowly becoming the player of old, until a game versus Cavalier in Park River's Holiday Tournament.

Halfway through the third quarter, while fighting for position to rebound, I was elbowed twice in the face. Blood poured from my nose. I rushed to the locker room to stop the bleeding, but it wouldn't stop. It flowed so much that I had to put tampons up my nose. They stopped the bleeding, so despite the embarrassment I returned to the game. I was not going to let a little pain keep me from playing the game I loved.

When I returned however, I was hesitant about playing physical, because I didn't want to get hit in the face again. I would shy away from going for rebounds or driving the lane. I knew I was hurting my team more than I was helping it, so I took myself out of the game, because I would rather see my team win than play.

After the game, I realized that I should not have gone back in the game at all, considering my nose had broken into nine pieces in my accident, and those elbows could have broken it again. Fortunately, that didn't happen. My parents agreed with me that the elbows to my face didn't break my nose or cause anything too serious, but we were soon to find out that it was much more serious than we had expected.

After the bloody nose, everything in my life changed. I started to become weak, had painful headaches, and became tired much faster than before. Everyday tasks became harder as each day passed. At night I was not able to sleep, so in class I had a hard time staying awake. Practice after school became exhausting.

I felt weak while running, but I thought it was just a phase, so I fought through it each day. I didn't tell my parents at first, because I was afraid they might make me stop playing basketball until I was back to normal again.

I kept playing until a game versus Midway-Minto showed my parents, coaches, and myself just how serious my condition actually was. In that game, even the adrenaline of being able to once again play the game I loved couldn't keep me going. At the start of the game, I could barely run up and down the floor. On a fast break, I trailed on Jay's left side when he gave me a perfect pass under the basket for an easy layup and two points. I felt so weak and uncoordinated that I thought I needed to put a lot of force into my shot just to get it to the basket, but instead the ball awkwardly sailed over it. After I shot and missed, I felt physically and emotionally defeated and couldn't even run back down the court to get back on defense.

My parents noticed and told the coaches to take me out. At that moment, I had to face the fact that something was seriously wrong. My mind told me to keep going, but my body would not move. I knew I had to let go of basketball; I was unable to play anymore.

After the game, I told my parents what had been going on, and they were very concerned. Things were not looking good.

The morning after my game, I couldn't get out of bed. My body felt like it was shutting down. My parents told me to stay home for the day. We assumed I had worked my body too hard too soon, and it just needed a break to regain some strength.

When I woke up the next morning, I didn't feel better, but much worse. I could hardly move my body to even get out of bed, let alone go to school. My parents told me to stay home again and wait to see how I felt in the next few days.

Every time I tried to go to bed, my head felt like it was spinning at a hundred miles per hour, making it difficult to sleep, so I walked around like a zombie all day. I constantly felt dizzy with a bad headache and my double vision was coming back. As a few more days passed, the symptoms escalated to the point of pure exhaustion. I didn't tell my parents, because I didn't want them to worry any more than they already were, and just in case I snapped out of this phase.

However, one night when I was home alone, I became so weak and light-headed that I collapsed on the kitchen floor. My head took the brunt of the hit. I'm not sure how long I laid there, but I woke up very scared and in shock.

The next day, my parents called my doctors to tell them about my collapse and what was going on. The doctors said for me to keep resting for a few more days before I came in for an appointment. But my symptoms increased, causing not only physical trauma but emotional pain as well.

While I was lying in my bed one day, a sad, eerie feeling overtook me. I didn't know where it was coming from, but I felt like I was in a different world where I was cold, sad, and lonely. It was a very dark place with no hope and only sadness. My emotions went on overload and I started crying. I didn't understand what was going on, and I continued to cry harder and harder until my parents heard me and rushed in to see what was happening.

They tried to settle me down, to tell me everything was going to be okay. As I felt their hands holding me, I realized what was happening. These were the same two people who had found me in the field, and now I was reliving my car accident. I felt the intense sadness of knowing I was going to die without saying goodbye to my family; the loneliness of being by myself until my parents found me; the feeling of being covered in half-frozen mud; the pain of my shattered face, crushed leg, and beat-up organs; the dark feeling of death upon me with no hope in sight.

After about ten minutes, I finally quit crying and was able to talk again. It was a new and scary experience for me, and it was weird to actually remember my accident and all the different feelings that I had at the time. My parents told me the doctors warned them that flashbacks may or may not happen. They did. They would again.

At that point, I had missed more than a week of school, but there was no telling how much longer it may be, because the doctors didn't know what was wrong with me, and my symptoms kept getting worse. A month earlier, everything seemed perfect; I was getting good grades and starting on the basketball team. Now, I had to quit basketball and couldn't go to school. I was really starting to become impatient in knowing what God's plan was for me, and why this was happening after I had come so far in my recovery. It seemed as if a dark cloud had started to cover me, but I was soon to experience a day much darker than the rest.

# Bent But Not Broken

*The Lord is close to the brokenhearted and saves those who are crushed in spirit.*

Psalm 34:18 (NIV)

With my life turned upside down, I started to feel sorry for myself again. I became mad at God for everything, even though He had saved my life, and I fell into depression. I had worked so hard to get it all back after losing it the first time, and now, I had lost it all when it was in my grasp. I missed playing basketball, seeing my friends, and simply being a normal teenager like I used to be.

While I fell deeper into depression because of the pain from my many setbacks, my idea of life started to become unclear. I did not understand why these things were happening to me or why I should try to hang on and keep going. The pain was slowly engulfing me into a darkness that I seemingly could not escape. All my emotions came to a breaking point while I was looking at myself in the mirror one day in my room. I started to hate the person I was looking at and question whether I wanted to live any longer with all pain I was feeling. Tears poured down my face because I never thought it would come to this, but my hope was gone. At that moment, out of frustration and anger, I turned around and banged my head against my bed frame repeatedly until my mom came in moments later. She found me in tears, and realized the situation.

After my flashback of what I felt in the field, I had seen many doctors, but no one could figure out what was wrong with me. I had now hit it an all-time low and was taken to the Psychology Ward at Altru Hospital. While in the hospital, I was constantly observed and questioned along with other patients to make sure we were mentally stable. After spending a few hours there and seeing and hearing the kids who had come there before me, I knew I did not belong there. I realized that even though God had already saved my life twice before, He had brought me here to mentally and spiritually wake me up and save my life once again. It seemed as if the darkness that once engulfed me had now been overtaken by a light that gave me hope and strength.

Now after I spent a night in the hospital, a doctor who had been reviewing my previous test results and symptoms finally figured out what was wrong with me. I was diagnosed with post-concussion syndrome, which is a disorder that occurs after a concussion and causes many symptoms such as headaches, dizziness, fatigue, and personality changes.

This new syndrome was due not only to the severe brain injury that I sustained, but also the overwhelming amount of work and pain I had put my body through to play basketball again, and the two elbows I took to the face in the holiday tournament. The doctor said I came back far too fast and should have done it slowly with many more precautions.

There were no treatments for post-concussion syndrome, so I just had to be patient and wait for my brain and body to heal. I also learned that it would take another another year for my body to fully heal from my accident.

I wasn't thrilled with all the news, but glad to finally know what was wrong with me. I just wanted to see my friends again and get healthy enough to play basketball next year, but the only thing I could do now was go home, pray, rest, and wait for everything to heal.

The day I got out of the hospital, I surprised my friends in the locker room before their game. It was like old times being in the locker room before games. It made me sad that I couldn't run out there with them, but motivated me even more to come back stronger for next year.

At home, I was very weak and had little motivation to do anything—especially not all the homework I'd missed in the last month. As the days turned into weeks, I was still not strong enough to go back to school, and I was falling farther behind. Then the decision came that I would have to quit school for the year and do it over again next year.

Right away when I heard this, I called my best friend, Ian Myrdal, to tell him the bad news. When Ian started school in Park River in fifth grade, many of the kids in our class didn't welcome him, just because he was the new kid in school. Kids would try to bully him and threaten to beat him up. One day, I heard that some kids were planning on riding the same bus with him after school to beat him up. I was furious when I heard this, so I told him that I would ride the bus with him and protect him. Ever since that day, we have been best friends.

Leaving my class was one of the hardest things that I have ever had to do. I wouldn't graduate with the friends that I grew up with and loved dearly. Many nights

I would stay up and look at old pictures of my friends and me, reminiscing about the best times that I had with them. I felt I was getting left behind and was scared that my new class would not accept me. Even though I would still be in the same school as my friends next year, I knew it would be much different because I would not be in the same classes as they were. My parents tried to tell me that everything would be fine and that my grandpa had repeated a year in high school because of rheumatic fever and everything turned out fine for him, so it would for me too. I appreciated that they tried to make me feel better, but it was too hard to think about.

The only positive part of quitting school was that I could now stay home and rest to recover for school and basketball next year. This time during my recovery, I promised my parents that I would not push myself as hard, and I would be smart with my body, so I didn't push it to the point of complete exhaustion again.

By mid-February, I finally started feeling stronger and was allowed to ride the bus to the rest of the away games that season. That made my life much more enjoyable.

## Spring 2008

Through the spring, my dad took care of me at home because my mom was back at her job teaching. Since I was not helpless like after my accident, my dad could work on the farm and periodically check on me. He made breakfast and lunch for me every day, and usually it was eggs, meat, and milk to give me the protein I needed to build my body back up.

My dad and I talked every day about life in general and the Bible. He understood that I felt bad about the situation I was in, but reminded me that without God I would not have been alive, and that He has a better plan for me than I had for myself. After all of our talks, we had become closer than I had ever dreamed possible before my accident. My dad had truly become one of my mentors. Even though I was not happy that I was in the accident, it started to feel more like a blessing than a tragedy, because it brought us to be best friends.

That spring, I drove by myself for the first time since my accident. Before that, I would either have Andrew with me going into school, or my mom or dad any other time. I was very hesitant while driving after my accident, so driving alone for the first time was a big deal for me. Plus, this was not just a simple trip from home to town. I was driving our Tahoe from Fargo, ND, back to Park River, which is a two-hour drive. The drive was going perfectly until a huge buck jumped out from the ditch and hit me, totaling the front of the Tahoe. Thankfully, I was wearing my seatbelt, so I was not injured. While I was sitting there, though, the memories of my accident rushed through my head, and terrified me. I could not believe that this happened on my very first time driving alone, but I guess that is the way God scripted it.

By May, I was much healthier and seemed to be over my post-concussion syndrome. I started to work out again, but very slowly this time. I would go up to the weight room at the high school and lift with my friends who were in track, so I could see them as much as possible, since I was not in school anymore. I was shocked to see that I had lost pretty much all of the strength that I had worked for last summer. I had also lost fifteen pounds while recovering, so I knew that I had a lot of work to do again to come back for basketball next year.

Mentally, I was much healthier since I was feeling better physically. With time, I had accepted that I had to do my junior year over and there was nothing that I could do about it, so I tried to think about the positives like being able to play basketball for two more years, becoming closer to my dad, but most of all, the fact that I knew God was with me and that He would once again motivate me to keep working and help me overcome any doubt or obstacle that was in the way of my returning for next year's basketball season.

## Summer 2008

Throughout the summer, I worked hard, but also paced myself because I didn't want to overwork my body again. I started running and using jump soles, which are specialized shoes that are made to help you improve your vertical. I would run a mile during the day and do different exercises with my jump soles at night. I did many different kinds of pushups per day to work my body harder as the summer went on, to increase my strength and endurance in my upper body. I increased the miles per day and the intensity in using the jump soles month by month and by the end of summer; I felt much stronger and faster, but I knew I still had a lot of work to do.

My summer was overall much better than the last, since I was much more independent and stronger. I could drive and go more places since I was stronger, and also do more work on the farm, which helped me gain back strength. My mom and dad again were there the whole summer, motivating me and keeping me positive. Bible camp that summer was also much more fun because I was able to do most of the things my friends were doing.

## Fall 2008

Starting out the school year, I knew it was going to be a big adjustment for me being in a new class, but I honestly did not know what to expect. Compared to last year, I could tell that I was stronger physically and also mentally than last year, which made it much easier to pay attention in class and lift weights after school. My goal was to return to the same weight and regain the strength that I had before my accident, so I could be the same player I used to be. I knew I could do it, because after I defied the odds to come back and play last year; I felt that anything was possible. This time, though, I wanted to work my hardest to get in the best shape possible, but also stay healthy and have no setbacks. It was not going to be easy, but to play basketball alongside my teammates in pursuit of our lifetime dream made the pain more than worth it.

At one point, my friends asked me to join football, but the doctor said it would be too risky, because of the injury to my brain last year and the post-concussion syndrome in the spring. I was hoping to help out my friends and play football alongside them like old times; however, I knew I still had basketball to look forward to, which was my main focus.

My social life was really tough at the beginning of the year, because even though I got along with everyone, I still felt as if I was alone or an outcast and missed being with my class like old times. Since I was not in their classes or in football anymore, I didn't see or talk to my old classmates as much as I used to. And even though I knew most of the people in my new class, I didn't have the relationships that I had with my old class.

Fortunately, I did have one friend already in my new class. Cole Solseng had worked on our farm that summer, doing the everyday chores of milking, feeding, or bedding down the cows with me. It really helped to have someone in my class that I was already friends with. Also, during football season, I became friends with a guy who is one of my best friends to this day. Since he also was not in football, Evan Koenig would come up to the weight room every day and lift with me. Considering, we lifted together every day; we got to know each other pretty well and quickly became good friends.

As it was coming close to basketball season, things were looking good for me. I felt comfortable enough to talk to almost anyone in my new class now, so going to school was much more enjoyable. And since football was done, there was more time to hang out with my old classmates. I was again on the A honor roll; my social life was much healthier; and I was in the best physical condition since my pre-accident sophomore year.

The thought of going to State, and how happy my teammates and I would be, motivated me and helped me fight through the pain during workouts each day. Since my body was much stronger than last year, I was able to work more on my basketball skills like shooting, dribbling, and post moves. I continued to go to Cenex every day after each workout to buy my four quarts of chocolate milk, blueberry muffin, and a bag of jerky.

### WINTER 2009

When basketball practice started, I was 180 pounds and much stronger than last year. The expectations for our team were very high, since we had taken second in the region last year. We had great depth and were rated number one in the state. Going to State had been our dream since we started playing together in second grade. I was thrilled to be back to help my friends and teammates reach our lifetime goal and ready to take the challenge head on.

The practice season started off really well for me as I excelled in all of the running and conditioning drills, but as we started playing scrimmage games I noticed that something was off. I was not comfortable yet, and I was also having a lot of trouble keeping up with the fast pace of my teammates. I had trouble catching crisp passes from my teammates, but I just thought that it would take time to adjust. However, there was more to it than I thought.

When I told my dad about what was going on, he explained that the doctors had said that since I had post-concussion syndrome on top of the brain injury in my accident, it would now take even more time for my brain to fully heal. The doctors were not sure how long or how much it would affect my hand-eye coordination. This explained why I was having trouble, but I was not going to let it get me down. I just had to keep playing and adjusting to the high pace.

Before the first game, I was very nervous, because now it was real, and I wanted to live up to the expectations that I had set for myself. I struggled to keep up with the fast pace of the game, but I knew I had all season to improve. After the game, the coaches suggested I play junior varsity along with varsity, so I could get more playing time. Hopefully that would help improve my hand-eye coordination and help me adjust to the flow of the game so I would be at my maximum potential at the end of the season when it meant the most. At first, I didn't want to play junior varsity because it felt like a downgrade, but I agreed and started to play three quarters in each game. With the increased playing time, my coordination drastically improved in just a few games. But it also brought increased pain.

I didn't tell anyone about an injury I'd been dealing with for months. I honestly had no idea what the injury was or how I got it. I started feeling an extreme pain from my right wrist to my elbow when I lifted weights and worked on my shooting form after school, but I just hoped it would heal without any treatment. At first, I was planning on playing through the pain, because the last thing I wanted to do was quit playing again. But it became worse and got to the point where I couldn't bear the pain anymore. One day when I was feeling my arm where it hurt, I heard and felt a crunch inside my arm, and felt more pain than I could take. I knew then something was seriously wrong with my arm, so I decided to tell my parents and coaches about it. They immediately referred me to the doctor.

I had severe tendonitis throughout my arm, and at first the doctor thought it needed surgery, so that it wouldn't get any worse. Thankfully, surgery wasn't necessary but I did have to wear a brace and stop playing basketball for at least the next month or until it healed fully. To me, that was heart-breaking news, especially since I knew it was my fault that I was in this situation. During the previous summer, I had started shooting and working on my shot at my house on the cement slab my dad gave us when I was younger. I would shoot for a few hours, and I did that up to basketball season on most days. Also, after taking it slowly at the beginning in the weight room, I had started pushing my body much harder too soon, because I thought that my body could handle it this time, since I was much stronger than last year. Even though my arm started to hurt while I lifted, I thought it was nothing serious and that I wouldn't make any progress unless I fought through the pain. Consequently, once again I had pushed my body too hard from the constant shooting and vigorous lifting, and I had to pay the price.

I knew I should have ultimately felt blessed that God saved my life multiple times, but I felt it was unfair that my hard work went to waste and only hurt me, when it was supposed to help me. I just wanted to be normal again like before my accident, so I would be able to play basketball with my friends. Once again, I questioned why this happened to me and what God's plan was for me this time. However, I would soon experience a pain far greater than the pain in my arm.

# A Blessing In Disguise

*"For I know the plans I have for you," declares the Lord,*
*"plans to prosper you and not to harm you, plans to give*
*you hope and a future."*

Jeremiah 29:11 (NIV)

Even though I was hurt and couldn't play, the season was
not going to stop for me. I wanted to make sure that when
my arm was fully healed I was in game form and ready
to go, so I continued to run with the team every practice
and also some extra at the end to make up for the running when they scrimmaged in practice or played in the
real games.

As the weeks turned into a month, I could tell that my
arm had fully healed and I was ready to play again. I started slowly on junior varsity, but hoped I would be back to
playing varsity soon.

It felt good to be back again playing with the boys that
I grew up with, since we knew how to play with each other so well. I knew that I still had a ways to go before I was
back to the player I used to be, but I was definitely on the
right track and I was not going to give up.

By the time the junior varsity tournament rolled
around, I had vastly improved and back to the player I once
was. After an above-par performance in our last game of

the tournament, the coaches were convinced that I was ready to return to full-time varsity.

In my first game back, we were playing Fordville-Lankin and I was beyond excited to be back full-time with my life-long teammates and friends. After halftime, the game did not look good for us and we were losing. I knew I had to step up and control the rebounding on both the defensive and offensive ends. However, on one particular play when I was going in for a rebound, I was hit by an elbow. Before the season, I had a specially fitted mask made for me, so I could withstand hits to the face. Unfortunately, on this occasion, the elbow missed the mask and hit my left temple.

The elbow left me stumbling to the bench, but it all happened so fast that I wasn't sure what was wrong. I remember going straight to the end of the bench and I just sat there with my head down, staring at the floor. I felt confused as to what I was doing and feeling. It was as if I was sinking into blank space, and my body had lost every ounce of energy to move. Our assistant coach, Mr. Omdahl, immediately came down to me to see what was wrong and told me to put my head up and open my eyes. After he saw my eyes, he knew I had a concussion, and some of the bench players helped me get to the locker room. I felt exhausted and kept falling asleep, but the coaches kept waking me and asking me questions, because if I fell asleep, I could possibly fall into a coma.

They kept this up until the paramedics arrived and carried me on a stretcher into the ambulance. They transported me to Altru Hospital in Grand Forks where I would be evaluated. After some tests, it was confirmed that I had had a concussion, but no crack to the skull, which was good news. However, lying there in the hospital after hearing that I had another concussion, I was physically and emotionally drained, and ready to give up on my dream that I had worked for so long and hard. My parents tried to comfort me with the positive news that my skull was not cracked, but I was too defeated to listen. I tried to give them a smile or two, but they understood why I was sad.

As I continued to lie there with my eyes closed, speechless, tears filled my eyes and rolled down my cheeks. In my head, I started asking God, *Why? Why now, during my very first game back when everything was going perfect for me?* I did not understand His plan or why this was all happening to me when I had worked so hard to come back each time. I felt like I was in another world actually talking to God, but when I finally came back to reality, I realized that my mom was holding my hand, just like she did the whole time I was in the hospital after my accident. That gave me the heart-warming feeling that she was there for me again, and it also put hope back in my heart. It would have been really easy for me to give up on my dreams at that moment, but whatever God's plans were for me, I knew that giving up was not something that He would plan on or want me to do.

The doctors told me that I would be out for at least a month to heal from my concussion because of my past concussions. My goal was to stay in game shape and be ready to play whatever role the coaches gave me during the playoffs. As the season continued, I kept running to stay in shape and used different drills to work on my hand-eye coordination. After playing in countless tournaments and games together while growing up, my teammates were all like brothers to me, and I simply wanted to help them win and reach our childhood dreams.

The playoffs were coming up quickly and I realized I

had to make a difficult decision. Should I start playing again and risk another concussion this soon that could end my career, or wait until next year to give my head the time it needed to fully heal? I wanted to play again as soon as I could, but my parents wanted me to wait until next year, because they were afraid that I would get another concussion. I didn't know what to do, but it seemed as if something inside my heart kept telling me to wait. I thought about it and realized that I didn't know the plays that well, so I would be lost out there. I wasn't ready for the high speed, and had no more junior varsity games to help me prepare. I had one year left, and I could be putting that in jeopardy if I did play. I also knew this would be the last time that I would be able to play with the guys I grew up with, so this was a very hard decision for me. I decided to take my parents' advice and wait until next year, because I knew it was the right and smart choice for me. If I did end up getting hurt, I would never have forgiven myself.

It was really hard to sit on the sidelines not being able to help my teammates, especially at the end of the last game, because I knew that this was the end for us as teammates. I felt selfish knowing that I had a year of basketball left, but I knew I had made the right choice, no matter how bad it hurt. Sadly, my teammates did not reach our lifelong dream, but they gave it a valiant effort. And even though we lost, there was one thing that no one could take away from us—the memories that we had together growing up and playing basketball. Some of my greatest life memories have been made on the basketball court with those guys.

I decided to join track that year and run long distance, so I would continue to run and be in the best shape possible next year in basketball. Koenig also decided to join track with me, so we lifted after we ran every day at practice. By the end of the school year, I was physically in the best shape of my life, but my emotional state was not so strong.

As the year drew to an end, it became harder to handle the feeling and idea of my classmates graduating and leaving to start a new life. Again, I felt as if I was being left behind, even though they couldn't help it. Most of all, it hurt to think about life without my best friends in school next year. The days before graduation were the hardest, with them talking about the excitement of graduating and practicing their formal walk to the stage. In my head, I would always think that I should be walking up there with them, but for some reason; God had a different plan for me.

After graduation, my feelings returned to normal, and I again focused on getting ready for next year's basketball season. I knew it would be my last year, so I wanted to make it my best.

During the summer, I was finally one-hundred percent physically healthy, so I returned to working hard on the farm all summer. Koenig worked there with me all summer, so that made working there every day a lot of fun. Along with farm work, I worked out every day on my break with the weights that my Uncle Daniel gave me. In the evenings, I would use my jump soles to work on my vertical. Overall, it was a very different summer because I was fully healthy for the first time in two years and I was able to work and lift without any restrictions. Still, I didn't play in any real games during the summer, because I didn't want to risk the chance of getting hurt before the season even started.

## FALL 2009

Toward the end of the summer, I was nervous for school to start because it would be the first time without most of my old classmates around. Even though I thought it would be a tough year without them, little did I know that God would bless me with new friends that would make it the most memorable school year of my life.

Paul Dusek, who was from Grafton, quickly became one of my best friends, and along with Koenig helped me adjust to my new grade and made my senior year a memorable one. Whenever I was not in Park River on the weekend, I was usually in Grafton hanging out with Paul and other friends. Paul and I met at Park River Bible camp a year earlier and had the same beliefs and interests. Hanging out with him strengthened my faith because we would frequently talk about the Bible.

Along with gaining a good friend, I also regained another in Michael Schildberger, who has been one of my best friends throughout my life. While all my friends in my old class went off to college, he stayed home in Park River to continue working on our farm, which he had done for the previous three years. He staying home was a true blessing to me, because it gave me a familiar face to see every day and a longtime best friend, who helped me cope with the new changes in my life.

In the first part of the year, Evan and I continued to lift and shoot together after school every day to get ready for basketball, because we had our own plan of making a push in the playoffs. I took working out very seriously every day after school and would sometimes go up to the weight room and work on my vertical during lunch, just to get in an extra workout.

But as basketball season approached, Mr. Beckman, our principal, told me the bad news that I might not be able to play basketball anymore because, technically, I had already played in four high school seasons. I looked up to Mr. Beckman as a good friend. He is a very kind person with a similar sense of humor to mine, so we would joke around when Evan and I visited him in his office during open campus. For April Fool's Day, Evan and I decided to pull a prank on Mr. Beckman and tell him that his pickup was stolen. We were going to pretend to be the Grand Forks police and tell him that we had found his pickup in Grand Forks, stolen from his garage in Park River. We hoped he would fall for it and come home to realize that it was a prank when he found an April Fool's note that we had taped on the door of his garage. We had even written up a script so we wouldn't forget what to say when we called him. During our study hall, we went into the locker room and I called him with the script in hand. As soon as he answered, I started reading it.

After about ten seconds, he interrupted me and asked, "Ben, is this you?"

I had even spoken in a different voice, so he would have no clue it was me. However, he told us that it was too obvious because it was April Fool's, and he knew that the only two people who would do something like this to him were Evan and me.

Mr. Beckman volunteered to send a letter to the state to make a special exception to the four-year rule for me, because I had not finished the past two seasons due to my injuries. Thankfully, they accepted his request, which meant that I could play. I was thrilled when I heard the news, because it would have been devastating to not be able to play my last year, after I'd worked so hard to get to that point. It also felt good to have a principal who cared about me enough to go out of his way to help me achieve my dreams.

Before the regular season starts every year, we have a scrimmage, which is a practice game with another team. That year, we were playing Langdon. During the game, I could tell I was much more comfortable and confident than I had ever been before, since I was in the best shape of my life and my basketball skills were better than ever.

However, while I was dribbling the ball on the top of the key, an opponent tried to steal the ball and our heads collided. It hardly hurt and I was not affected at all by the hit, but at that moment, I questioned whether basketball was worth it.

After the scrimmage, I kept thinking about the bumping heads and just how easy it would be to get another concussion. I started to question if playing basketball was worth the possibility of being negatively changed for life. I couldn't believe I was actually thinking about quitting basketball after all the work I had put in to play it again, but something changed inside me and told me to be careful. Basketball was my passion in life, but I started to realize there is more to life than sports.

I talked to my dad about my feelings, and he agreed and was proud of what I was thinking. We discussed the whole situation and came to the conclusion that basketball was not worth getting another concussion, and that giving it up was the right choice. After our talk, it felt as if my fire to play basketball was gone. I thought back to the last two-and-a-half years and everything I had gone through—from imagining my dream of playing again and not giving up no matter what happened, to now quitting on my own terms. My dad made sure I realized I was not quitting; I was doing what was best for my future. It was hard to think about it like that, but the more I thought about it, the more I realized that even though I had not played in a full season since my sophomore year, I had achieved my dream of playing again and had done things that were thought to be impossible for me. Even though I still loved basketball, I knew this was the right decision.

The next morning, it was time to tell my coach about my decision, and it was definitely one of the hardest things I have ever done. While walking to talk to him, I kept turning around and second-guessing my decision. But in my heart I knew this was right, even though a part of me still wanted to play so badly.

As I finally walked in, my coach, Mr. Omdahl, knew right away that something was wrong. As I told him the news, I couldn't help but break down a little, since I was ending something I had played since I could first remember. I believed that God had a plan for me, but I didn't know what it was yet. And I knew I had to trust in it, even if it meant not knowing what the future held for me.

*Trust in the Lord with all your heart, and lean not on your own understanding; In all your ways submit to him, and he will make your paths straight (Proverbs 3:5-6 NCV).*

Life without basketball was definitely different and tough, because I wanted to be out there with my friends to help them win, but I knew in my heart that this was the right decision and part of God's plan for me. My good friend Evan knew how tough it was on me, so he dedicated his season to me and put my basketball number, twenty-one, on the inside of his shoe to symbolize that even though I was not playing anymore, I was still a part of the team. And even though I technically was not on the team, the school still let me ride on the bus with the team to all of the away games. I was considered by Mr. Scherr and Mr. Omdahl as another assistant coach because they knew how much basketball had meant to me. The team lost in districts, but on a bright note, Evan won "District Four's Senior Athlete Award."

Senior year turned into my favorite school year because of how close I became to my new classmates and how much fun I had with them every day. Towards the end of the school year, Carter Hunter and I were to be inducted into the Honor Society at the annual banquet. Usually, the banquet is a very formal event because it is an honor to be inducted, but we had an idea to make it a little more fun, and we got approval from Mr. Beckman and our English teacher, Mrs. Anderson, who was in charge of the ceremony. Each inductee had to pick a person to speak on their behalf, so Carter and I picked Evan. When it was our turn, the lights went out and the Chicago Bulls warm-up song starting playing, a spotlight shone around the gym, and Carter and I were inducted into the Honor Society with Evan introducing us like the starting line-up in a basketball game.

I went to senior prom with a new close friend, Courtney Rehovsky. It was easily my favorite prom of all time, considering I was able to spend it with all my new friends and classmates. And as graduation came closer, I also became closer to God, because I started to realize that being in this new class was truly a blessing. A part of me was changing and starting to really think about how much God had blessed me since my accident. So many things could have gone wrong, but didn't. How perfect everything was turning out to be. I started to become more thankful for everything I did have, instead of being sad because of the things I did not have, and to truly appreciate what God had done for me on April 6, 2007.

I reflected my feelings in a paper I wrote in English that was to describe an event that happened in our lives. I wrote about my accident and how precious life is and how I had learned not to take the little things in life for granted. My teacher, Mrs. Anderson, liked it and sent it into a competition and it was chosen to be put in high school English books nationwide.

As May started, the realization that I was finally going to graduate was surreal; and on May 23, 2010, that realization came true. It was an amazing feeling to walk up to get my diploma that day, remembering all of the obstacles I had to overcome and how far I had come since my accident. It was crazy to think that about three years before that, my life was almost taken, and even though I had survived, the doctors thought that I could be mentally and physically changed for life. Now three years later, I was graduating from Park River High School with honors, multiple scholarships, and a healthy mind and body. I had truly done things that seemed to be impossible, but only with God's help. Through all that He had done for me, I firmly started to believe that anything in life was possible with Him. It gave me a new positive outlook on life and became so much a part of me and my thinking that I decided to permanently imprint it on myself by getting the Bible verse, "Jesus replied, 'What is impossible with men is possible with God'" Luke 18:27 tattooed on my abdomen, so that I would never forget what He did for me as long as I live.

With high school and sports over, I figured my summer would be boring. However, that was far from true.

## SUMMER 2010

Even though my sports career was done, I still loved to work out; it had become a part of me since my accident. So I went into the weight room whenever I had time, since my parents also had me working hard on the farm every day. Trying to fit in lifting and working on the farm every-day was tiring at first, but I quickly adjusted.

In late June, I got my first break from work when Mr. Beckman took Evan, Cole, and meI to two Minnesota Twins games in Minneapolis, MN. Earlier in the year, he had told us that it would be our graduation present, which was absolutely amazing. The whole trip was a blast and a memorable experience; however one part of the trip will be a memory that Evan and I will never forget.

Before we left Park River, we all had tickets for the first game, but decided to buy tickets in Minneapolis before the second game. However, we could not find any tickets that were at a reasonable price, so we bought standing- only ones. This meant we could only stand to watch the game, but they were also the cheapest ones available. Evan and I did not want to stand the whole time, so we decided to bend the rules like in high school and sneak down to the lower deck by the field for a good view of the game. While the security guards weren't looking, we snuck down by the field to get autographs from the players and find good seats. We were fortunate enough to get autographs from Carl Pavano and Denard Span, but we had a strong feeling that we would be kicked out of our seats.

It was still half an hour before the start of the game, so there were plenty of open seats at the moment, but we knew it would be a sell-out that day, since it was the first season in their new stadium and they were playing their division rival, the Detroit Tigers. We started out sitting about fifteen rows up, but as the seats kept filling up, we kept moving farther down towards the field, until we were in the first row by the first base line with only two seats open next to us. We had a feeling that we should move over to the two empty ones, so we went with our guts and did that. A minute later, two people came and sat in the two seats that we just moved from, so we had nowhere else to go. We were now just waiting for someone to come down and kick us out, but by the fifth inning, we realized that we had found the only two seats that were open in that section, and they happened to be front row seats. We were in shock that we were this close. In the seventh inning Johnny Damon was up for the Tigers and hit a high foul ball that seemed to be coming right for us. As it came closer, I realized that it was dropping right on top of me. Evan had a glove, so he tried to catch it. However, out of nowhere the Twin's shortstop, Orlando Hudson, dove into our laps to make the catch.

After the game, Evan and I could not believe that we just sat front row, got autographs, and had Orlando Hudson jump into our laps when we were supposed to have been standing only in the upper deck. Later on, we discovered that we had made Sportscenter's top ten plays when Hudson made that catch. At first, Mr. Beckman did not believe Evan and me when we told him all that had happened, until he saw us on Sportscenter that night on the Top Ten plays. For my former principal, but most of all, my friend, to do something like that for us was unbelievably generous and easily one of the most memorable experiences of my life, but there were many more to come.

# A New Beginning

*He said to them, "Go into all the world and preach the good news to all creation...."*

Mark 16:15 (NIV)

That summer was my last year at Bible camp. Knowing that it was my last year was very sad because it was my second home and was where I had made some of my best friends and memories. Also, since it was my last year as a camper, I wanted to make sure it was my most fun and memorable one. It was not only my most memorable week at camp, but was a turning point in my life.

It started out just like any other week at camp, but as it continued, I started to feel something inside me that I had never felt before. That year's main message at camp was making God the foundation of your life, and for some reason, it really hit home for me. During high school, after my accident, I thought that I was living a righteous life and trying to stay close to God for the most part, but I never would let God take control of my life and be my foundation. I believed that He was real, but I was not close enough to Him and did not trust Him enough to let Him lead me.

I also believed that God had saved my life, but I still

didn't know why. I had always felt thankful inside for Him saving me, but never truly felt close to Him in my heart. However, while we were singing camp songs one day, I felt a true closeness to God for the first time. It was such an amazing feeling and so overwhelming that I had to sit down to hide the tears. Without knowing it at the moment, it was a breakthrough in my life that spiritually changed me forever.

After we were done singing, I had the urge to tell the camp the story of my accident and how God had saved me and helped me do things that were supposed to be impossible. Wanting to speak in front of the camp seemed crazy to me since I had always hated public speaking. I would never tell it in the previous years at camp because I would get too nervous. But this year, something inside me told me I had to.

I would be telling my story that night at campfire. Without even thinking, I began praying that God would speak through me, and help me speak clearly and not forget anything. I prayed all day, up until it was time for me to speak. The weird part about that was that I had never prayed to God and truly believed that He would answer. I would pray sometimes before that, but I did it just because I felt like it was the right thing to do and did not truly believe that He would answer my prayers.

It was now time for me to go up and tell my story, and I was deathly nervous, but something inside me would not let me shy away. I went up and told the whole story, while speaking clearly the entire time and not forgetting anything. When I went back to sit down, I could not believe what I had just done. I realized that God had truly spoken through me and answered my prayers.

People must have liked it and it must have had an effect

on them because it made some people cry, and a day later one of the camp counselors asked me if I would come tell my story at her school, Jamestown College, next year. After saying it clearly that first time, I had confidence to tell it again, so I accepted.

While leaving camp that year, I realized that I had been changed, and that I was truly close to God for the first time. I wanted to make Him the foundation of my life and let Him lead me. I started praying every day for guidance and truly believed that He was there listening and would answer my prayers in one way or another. And I wholeheartedly realized and believed that the motivation to never give up physically, mentally, or spiritually after my accident did not come from myself; it came straight from God, who carried me through it all.

## Fall 2010

As college was only days away, I was excited to start something new, but also sad to leave behind everything in my life that I had known—most of all, my family. Since my accident, I had become very close to my family after everything we had been through together. I had formed a special bond with my mom because of the time we spent together in the hospital and at home during my recovery. She was there praying for me and holding my hand every day in the hospital, and she showed me unfailing love and motivated me at home.

My dad and I had also become very close in the years following my accident. Before, we were often mad at each other, because of my complaints about working on the farm. At times, we were so mad that we would barely talk to each other. However, my attitude about working on the farm changed. While I was in the hospital, I would have given anything to be on the farm working again, rather than being in a bed all day. With my new attitude, I was much easier to deal with and we talked all the time. After I came home from the hospital, the memories of him coming into my room every morning before he went to work to check on me and motivate me to keep fighting were imprinted in my head.

As for my little brother, Andrew, it was terribly hard to leave him. I felt as if I was leaving him behind. Andrew and I had always been somewhat close, but after my accident, we had formed a bond as brothers that could never be broken. Knowing that he could have been in a grave if he was in the car with me during my accident made my love for him multiply to no end. I cared about him as much as any human being possibly could, so it made it extremely hard for me to leave him.

I was attending the University of North Dakota, which is located in Grand Forks, ND, and only an hour away from home. I was planning on majoring in History, getting a degree in education, and a minor in coaching and possibly attending law school after I graduated. My sister also lived in Grand Forks, so that made the move much more comfortable, knowing that I had a family member close by.

When the day came, while I was leaving down the driveway, it was hard to keep driving as I remembered all of the good memories with my family and everything we had been through since my accident. It was probably the slowest I had ever driven out of my driveway. But after a bit, I was finally on the highway and ready to start a new chapter in my life.

I realized quickly how different it was going to be from living at home and being in high school. The first morning waking up in my dorm made me realize just how much I missed home and my family; it was the first time I woke up to go to school and I did not see my mom, dad, brother, or sister. It was truly a rude awakening.

I'd met my roommate Reilly Mathiason through Dusek during high school. Reilly was a great roommate, and since we had known each other previously, it was an easy adjustment living with him. College was a lot different from high school, since I sometimes had only a couple of classes each day and a lot of free time.

Although there were some good changes, there were also some negative ones that I had to deal with. With college, the temptations of drinking, immoral behavior, and sexual enticements became harder to resist, because they are much more common and accepted than in high school. Many of the students at college began drinking and partying as soon as they arrived, which I was not used to, since I steered clear of that in high school, because I had the luxury of having friends who did not party and parents who always kept me in line. There was a part of me that wanted to go out and join everybody because it did sound like fun, but I was on a mission to keep close to God and I knew that going out to party would only lead me away from Him.

Starting out, I only knew a few people who went to college there, so I spent most of my days going to class, working out at the wellness center, and doing homework or watching TV in my room. I figured working out or staying in my room would also make it easier to stay away from all of the temptations, but it became very lonely, because Reilly was in track and often at track meets or practice.

One Friday night, it became too hot in my dorm room to study, so I went out to the lounge where it was much cooler. While I was studying, a group of four guys and one girl came down the hallway. I recognized that two of the guys were in my wing, only a few doors down; but I had never met them, so I just kept studying. As they were walking past me, they all stopped next to me and one of the guys asked me if I had been in a fight because of the scar I had around my eye.

I explained to them that it was actually from a car accident and told them the story of what had happened, and the miracles that God had performed to save my life. After meeting Andy Peden, Anders Peterson, Josh Mellem, Myles Severson, and Brooke Hatlestad that night, they quickly became some of my best friends. I began hanging out with them every day and began to meet many more people, including other guys in our dorm wing. As we got to know each other, we soon became a very close-knit group of friends and called ourselves the "Walsh Bros," since we lived in Walsh Hall.

As the year progressed, the story of my accident became a popular topic of discussion because of the miracles that had happened, and it also had a positive impact on anyone who heard it. It became enjoyable for me to tell it to anyone who asked to hear it, because I knew it would strengthen their faith. After telling it to many people at UND and going to speak at Jamestown College, I started to wonder why God had saved me, and if this was why—to share my story and help people with their faith. Soon after, He showed me something that would change me forever and give me a hint as to why He saved my life.

# Alive For A Reason

*And we know that in all things God works for the good of those who love him, who have been called according to his purpose.*

Romans 8:28 (NIV)

On October 3, 2010, I took a girl to a University of North Dakota men's hockey game. I liked this girl, so the last thing I wanted to do was mess up and embarrass myself somehow. Everything was going perfectly until I was taking her home. While we were driving on the interstate, I started feeling weird and started crying, and could not stop. At the time, I had no idea why I was crying so I felt very embarrassed, especially because it was in front of the girl I liked. She tried consoling me and asked what was wrong, but I could not give her an answer, because I had no idea. Finally, we made it to her house and I dropped her off. At that point, I was confused and embarrassed, considering I had cried in front of her for about twenty minutes, but did not know why. After that, I just wanted to get the day over with, so I went home and went to bed.

The next morning was just like any other morning. I got up, brushed my teeth and showered, but I had this very strange image in my head. At first, I figured it was just something I had thought up by myself, but as the day went on, the thought kept playing over and over again exactly the same way. I then realized it was not a thought I made up; it was a memory.

I thought about how my crying last night was just like during my first flashback, and realized that this was my second flashback. The difference between this one and the first one was that in the first one, I had remembered something that happened while I was alive. However in this one, I remembered what happened when I had stopped breathing in the field.

The first thing I remembered was standing in the field where I was viewing my lifeless body that laid ten feet in front of me. The world that I was looking at was colorless. It all seemed gray to me. I had a new body, so I had no more pain, and I was clean without the blood or mud that I had endured when I was alive.

I remembered thinking, after standing there for a few minutes trying to let it all sink in, *Wow, so this is what it is like to die.* I was literally in shock, knowing that I was actually dead. But I knew I could not remain here forever in the field with my dead body. I figured something had to happen. After what seemed to be about five minutes, something did happen that would change me forever.

A man came and stood about ten feet to the left of me, but this was not just any normal man. This man had brown wavy hair down to his shoulders. He was wearing a pure white robe that glowed and had a golden rope around his waist. I could not see his face because it was too bright. Trying to look at his face was like trying to look at the sun. He did not look at me or talk to me and did not even acknowledge that I was standing there. I could not believe this was happening right in front of me. I was not scared, though, just in awe of this person's presence.

After what seemed to be a few minutes of Him standing there, He put His hands out and lifted my lifeless body that lay in front of me off the ground about six inches. His hands were shining pure gold and gold light shivered out from underneath my dead body. I did know that this man was holy, and that he was there to help me. After about a minute, he put my body back down on the field, and just like that I was back in the real world with all the mud, blood, and pain. The only difference between before I stopped breathing and after I came back was that before I felt as if I had no hope of survival, but after I had a newfound hope that God would keep me alive no matter what happened or what obstacle was in my way, so I could tell this story someday to glorify His name.

After realizing that this flashback was a true memory and after actually seeing it, I became much more passionate about the opportunity of the second chance at life that God had given me. It amazed me to see how much He loved me by saving my life, which also made my love for Him much stronger. It also proved to me once and for all that God and the Bible are real and true. I did not have to ever wonder again if everything that I had been taught growing up was true or not. It was a great feeling to be able to live now without questioning my faith. I now had a desire to share my story to give people evidence that the Bible is true and to strengthen their faith, so they don't have to question their beliefs anymore and can join God and Jesus in Heaven one day. As much as I felt it in my heart to share the story God gave me, I questioned why this was happening to me and what God's plan was for me. Although I did not know my future, I believed everything happens according to His will, so I knew I had to trust and follow wherever He took me in life. I also questioned who that mystery man was who saved me. I thought it may be Jesus, but I was not sure.

Even though it was hard to tell anyone about my flash-back at first, because of how crazy it sounded, I finally told my parents about it. They were astonished, but told me to take it as a blessing and do with it what God told me. In my heart, I knew God wanted me to share it with others, so I told my friends at college about it. It really helped some of their beliefs, since they now had evidence that God is real. One of my friends, Josh, told me that he always had strug-gled with his faith because he did not know for sure if it was true, but after hearing about my story and flashback, he was convinced that God is real and Jesus is his true Sav-ior. It was the first time that he ever started a real relation-ship with God. He started going to church with me and still does to this day.

Even though I had seen something that changed me and my faith forever, I was still living in a world filled with temptation. As I got to know many more people at col-lege, it became much harder to stay away from the par-ty scene. There were times when I fell into that tempta-tion and went out and drank with my friends. I felt terrible about it and knew that it was not how God wanted me to live. At times, I felt as if I was losing my faith and growing away from Him, so I knew that I needed to keep my life on track, because falling away from God is the one thing that scared me the most in life.

God gave me a friend, Brock Nelson, to help me over-come the temptations and keep my faith strong. He was also a person whose faith was affected by my story, so he knew what kind of person I was and who I wanted to be. With that, he knew that in my heart, I did not want to dis-obey God. He was also a person who did not want to, so we would just stay in and hang out in the dorms while everyone else would go out. Having him there was big for me, because it gave me a good friend I could always hang out with who shared the same beliefs as I did.

After going through trials and low points with my faith and obedience to God through the year, I came out of the year with a strong relationship with God. I knew that I was alive for a reason, but I was still not sure why. I did know that He wanted me to share my story, and He gave me that opportunity again after I spoke at Jamestown College. I was asked to share it with a Bible study group at UND and I willingly accepted. I felt as if it was my duty to tell anyone who asked to hear it because I knew it could only help them spiritually.

I felt so strongly about it that I wanted to start counseling at Park River Bible Camp during the summer. Before that, I never really gave any serious thought to it, because even though it would be fun, it would be such a big commitment. But in my heart, I felt that God was calling me there to share my story.

I always wondered what my life would have been like if I had not been in that car accident and was able to finish out my career in sports. I still really missed basketball, especially when I went to the wellness center and saw everyone playing. However, even though I did not play anymore, God gave me something in return that I never saw coming.

# Remind Me Who I Am

*The Lord makes firm the steps of the one who delights in him; though he may stumble, he will not fall, for the Lord upholds him with his hand.*

Psalm 37:23-24 (NCV)

Late that year, my dad called and told me that he was talking to my old coach, Mr. Scherr, who said that he wanted me to be one of his assistant coaches next year and train the players in the weight room in the summer. I was so excited and thankful that I really didn't know what else to do, but sit there and thank God for the blessing He had given me. I could not believe that I was going to be back as a part of the game that I loved, and that God gave me this blessing since I could not play anymore. It was truly a dream come true.

## SUMMER 2011

Even though I missed all of my friends at college, I was very excited to be back home with my family. I started working on the farm right away when I got home, but that was okay because I did not mind working on the farm so much anymore and especially in the nice summer weather. My dad and I developed a plan for me to counsel at camp for a few weeks that summer, and the whole summer in years to come.

Starting in June, I began training the basketball team in the weight room and opened up the gym so they could scimmage or shoot around. Being able to coach these guys was great, because it would give me some experience at a young age, since I wanted to coach basketball as part of my career.

It was also a lot of fun for me to train those guys because they were projected to be last in the district, but I knew they had enough talent to get first. It reminded me of when everyone doubted me after my accident. Throughout the summer, I trained them pretty hard physically, but mostly mentally to get them to push themselves past their limits and believe in themselves, that they could win. Sometimes we were in the gym doing drills, shooting, or talking strategy about next season until almost midnight, so I knew that they were motivated and dedicated to win. It was also very cool being able to coach my little brother. That in itself was a true blessing. I was never able to play with him, but God gave me the opportunity to coach him. By the end of the summer, the guys' confidence had increased dramatically and were all looking forward to the upcoming season, so they could prove their doubters wrong.

Later on in the summer, I took a little vacation with my buddy, Derek Rodwell and his girlfriend, Paige Birmingham, to her family's lake cabin. While driving there, he and I had a great talk about our faith in Jesus Christ, and how my story had helped him come closer to God. After hearing that, it started to sink in that God wanted me to share my story with as many people as possible, but I couldn't just go up to people and start talking; I needed to be given the opportunity. So I began praying for God to put me in the right place at the right time to share it.

God began answering my prayers shortly after that at the bible camp during senior high week, when I told my story to the cabin my friend Paul and I were counseling. I was asked many other times throughout the summer by other counselors to come to their cabins to tell my story to their campers. Many times, I would be told how much it impacted the kids and their faith. It meant a lot to me that my story could inspire campers whose faith was weak, but just needed some evidence to help their faith grow and prove to them that the Bible is true and God is real.

As the summer was coming to an end, I was back on the farm working with my family, but it was almost time to go back to UND to start my sophomore year. That meant that I would have to leave my family again, who meant so much to me. It was always the hardest to see my mom's face as I was leaving the house and saying goodbye, so I would always need to go back to give her one more hug.

Going into college that year, I had one thing in mind and that was staying as close to God as I could and continuing to share my message when given the opportunity. I knew that this year was going to be even harder than the last to stay away from all of the temptations, because I was now living in a house with five guys, where we could do whatever we wanted, since we did not live in the dorms anymore. I tried to surround myself with things to remind me to live like Jesus would by putting up Christian posters in my room, listening to Christian music, and going to church regularly.

I began the year with a very close relationship with God and I felt like that would never change no matter who or what tried to break us apart. The main thing that kept me close to Him was the amount of praying I did, because it felt as if I was having a conversation with Him all day. Because of that, it was easy to resist all the temptation that surrounded me.

However, as time went on, I slowly talked to God less and less each day, and my strength to resist temptation became weaker. Eventually, I began to join in and drink a little bit with my friends on the weekends, because I did not think one drink was bad, since I was of age and I just wanted to socialize. I soon found out that one drink can turn into many faster than I realized. As the weekends continued, I started to drink a little bit more each time, until I was drunk. Many people did not see anything wrong with it, but I knew in my heart that it was not what God wanted me doing with my life, and I felt terrible about it.

One of my friends from school asked me to speak at a Bible study he went to each week, but I was hesitant because I felt as if I did not deserve to say anything about Jesus or the Bible because of how I had been living. While talking to my good friend Josh Mayo, the topic of my speaking came up. I told him that I didn't think I should speak and the reason why. His response was something I have never forgotten. He told me that if I thought that I couldn't speak because I had been sinning, then no one in the entire world would be able to say one word about Jesus or the Bible ever again, because no one is perfect. What he told me really hit home for me and changed my mind about not speaking, because the gospel would never be able to be talked about if everyone thought like I did, since everyone sins.

On December 22nd, I had to have surgery on the leg that was crushed in my car accident, because the new artery that had been put in five years earlier was now failing, and I had an aneurysm in it. I was very frustrated with this because I thought I was done with injuries from my accident. I could not work out now for two months, so I had to work extra hard to get back into shape once again. I also could not attend practices or games for a while, but finally after a month of resting, I was back at practice and games with the boys. I did not understand why God was putting me through more hardship, but I did know that I was extremely blessed to just be alive, so I could not complain.

## SPRING 2012

To end the season, we lost in the first round of regionals, which was a huge disappointment for our team. However, the season was still a success in my eyes, considering we had overcome the many doubts of others to place second in our district at the end of the regular season. It also proved to me once again that with God, all things are possible.

After the season was over, it was back to the less busy normal life and that opened up the door for temptation. As hard as I tried to stay away, I once again found myself slowing falling away, but even worse than last time. I was not only drinking at times, but my relationship with God was becoming weaker. I was losing who I was and was forgetting about the God, who had saved my life. I began to put my friends, girls, and worldly objects in front of Him, until one day when everything that I was missing in my life all came back to me.

A month earlier, when I was still coaching, a woman called me from the *Grand Forks Herald* and asked if she could do a story on me, because she heard about my story and that it was the five year anniversary of it that April.

I accepted because I figured it would be a great way to help many people with their faith, since it would be in the newspaper.

I was expecting the morning of April 6th that year to be much like a normal one, but it was everything but that. I knew that it was the anniversary and had not forgotten what God had done for me, but the passion that I had in my heart to serve Him earlier seemed to be gone. When I woke up that morning, the memory of that mystery man saving me in the field popped into my head and it seemed like something inside me turned my faith and passion for God back on.

I remember turning on my favorite Christian song at the time, "Remind Me Who I Am" by Jason Gray. Hearing that song really hit me hard and brought me completely to tears, because I knew that God did not save my life for me to be living like I was. I would tell people throughout the year about Jesus and my story when asked, and would stand up for my beliefs, but I realized that I was not always living what I was saying. I also knew that many kids and Christians, like my little brother, looked up to me, so I needed to be a good role model for them. I wanted to help people find Jesus and live like God wants us to, but whatever I said would never have any impact on people unless I backed it up by living it. It made me sick to think about how much I was disrespecting God by putting so many other things in front of Him, after He had graciously given me a second chance at life.

That morning, my heart was changed forever and I devoted my life to The Lord. I learned after all my ups and downs that He would never leave me and always love me no matter how many times I failed Him, and that meant a lot, because He was the only true constant in my life that

I could always count on to be there for me when I needed help.

Two days later, it was Easter and the day my story would come out in the newspaper. I woke up that morning to a few text messages from my friends telling me how much they liked the article, which was normal, but as the day went on, I started to get Facebook messages and text messages from people whom I did not know. Many of them would simply tell me how much the article helped them with their faith, even though they did not know me personally. By the end of the day, I had countless messages and phone calls from people thanking me for sharing my story. I never thought it would have that great an impact on people and was surprised with the number of people who reached out to thank me. It was a great feeling to know that it positively affected so many people.

Having my life fully back on track and knowing how God was using the story He gave me to impact so many people made me really excited to share it at the Bible camp this summer with all the campers. I knew it was never too early to give your heart and life to Jesus, and that my story could give them the evidence they needed to have the faith to live for Him. Simply, God had fully taken over my heart and He compelled me to do whatever I could to help people find Jesus.

### Summer 2012

After training the guys in the gym and working on the farm for half the summer, it was now finally time to start counseling at the Bible camp. My first week at the end of June was a lot of fun while learning the ropes and counseling, but my second week was a week that I would never forget. Our second week was Jubilee week and that's when campers with special needs would come for a few days to simply have fun and learn about Jesus. Those two days were challenging with the high responsibility we had as counselors to take care of them, but it was also a very humbling and heart-warming experience.

It was eye-opening to see how all the campers lived their lives, because even though they did not live the most normal lifestyle, they all seemed to be satisfied with what they did have in life, instead of being sad because of what they didn't have. It made me realize that even when I think I have a bad life at times or have a problem, it is nothing compared to what some of them go through on a daily basis. They are all truly amazing people who made me smile or laugh all day and taught me to appreciate my blessings instead of dwelling on my problems.

As the summer continued, things became more fun every week and I made friends that would last a lifetime. I was the counselor of Central Hill, which was right in the middle of North and South Hill, which were counseled by two of my best friends, Tyler and Paul. Since we were little, we had been going to camp together and had some of our best times there, so we wanted to make sure that all the campers had the best week of their lives. We entertained the campers by starting our own band, "The Belts," since we would carry a wrestling title belt on stage every time we had a concert.

Bible study and nightly devotions were my favorite times of each week, because that was when we all focused on the Bible and God, and had an in-depth conversation about them. Every week during a nightly devotion, I would tell all three hill cabins my story, or go to another cabin to tell it by the request of another counselor. I believed that this was the single most important thing that I could do for the campers each week, because it would give their faith a foundation to grow on, and God was calling me there to share it. Plus while sharing it, it strengthened my faith as well, which helped me grow closer to God and keep resisting the many temptations that I once struggled with.

*Be on your guard; stand firm in the faith; be courageous; be strong (1 Corinthians 16:13 NCV).*

Throughout the summer, I always felt the urge to share my story on a bigger scale where it could impact more people, so I gave it to God and prayed for opportunities. Towards the end of the summer, God answered that prayer. Missy Ohe, a mother of one of my campers, happened to be the radio host for a Christian radio station in Grand Forks and she asked me to be on the show in the fall to tell about my story after her son, Andrew Ohe, had told her about it when she came to pick him up at camp. I thought this was an amazing opportunity and blessing in itself, but God would soon show me an even greater story to share.

# A Secret Revealed

*"For God so loved the world that he gave his one and only Son, that whoever believes in him shall not perish but have eternal life."*

John 3:16 (NIV)

*FALL 2012*

One day, while I was driving back to Grand Forks from my house by Park River, God showed me something that answered a question that I had been asking Him for five years.

I don't know why, but I decided to take the road that I had crashed on five years earlier. As I came closer to the spot where I had crashed, tears began to run down my cheeks until I was in a full-out cry. This all seemed too familiar to me from the two previous times that I had flashbacks, so I slowed down and waited for God to show me something. Literally five seconds later, an image popped up in my head of a man extending his left arm to show me a city so incredibly beautiful that it literally took my breath away. It had massive walls and gates surrounding it that appeared to be made from an assortment of gorgeous jewels. The structures in the city resembled earthly buildings, but they seemed to be made out of a radiant material, which glowed brilliantly. The most amazing sight was the mountain in the distance that the city rested by and part way up on, which had a peak that gloriously shined with light all around it.

However, human words cannot fully describe what I saw for it's magnificence and beauty is purely too miraculous to entirely comprehend.

I quickly became overwhelmed with emotion because I realized after the image kept playing over in my head that the same man that had saved my life in the field five years earlier was now showing me Heaven, but this time, I could now see His face. It was a lot to take in all at once, but I knew what I was seeing was true and was a real memory.

As I kept crying, God kept showing me more and I started to remember previously walking up to Heaven's gates with this man on what seemed to be clouds. I still remember how soft the feeling was on the bottom of my feet, for it was the softest feeling that I had ever felt. While we were walking, He explained to me where I was, and that my time on earth was not up yet because God wanted me to go back and share my story with the world to help give people the faith they need to receive eternal life in Heaven someday. The man who saved me and walked with me never told me who He was, but as I walked with Him and recognized the kindness in His voice, I felt as if it was Jesus Christ, the Son of God. However, I will not know for certain who He was until I pass away and go to Heaven, but what I did and do know is that He was a Heavenly being and was sent by God to save my life, and share with me why I was given a second chance.

After sitting in the car for a while trying to take in everything that I had just seen, it dawned on me that I had just remembered what had happened to me when my lungs had collapsed on the operating table. It was an amazing moment in my life, because I now knew that Heaven is a real place and finally knew the answer to the question that God had kept hidden from me for years, why I was saved. I did not know how big of a part of my life that He wanted the sharing of my story to be, but I knew that He had already been opening doors and having me meet the right people by get the opportunity to speak about it and to share it on the radio in three weeks. With that in mind, I did not know what God had in store for me, but I was now ready for anything. I knew that His plan is perfect, so I had to trust whatever it was, for it would be the right one.

I have learned that life is always full of surprises and can change in an instant, so you have to be ready for anything at any time.

Two weeks later while meeting with Missy about the show, she gave me an idea that seemed almost impossible to me. She told me that I should write a book about my story and possibly become a motivational speaker as my career. Her idea seemed great, but writing a book seemed to be impossible, considering I was in college and I would also start coaching in November. I also had no idea how to get an editor or publisher, but to my surprise, she had connections with many people involved in the book business. And being a motivational speaker seemed amazing, but I needed to get my name and story out there to actually get an opportunity to start speaking, plus I already had my own aspirations of coaching basketball one day.

On my way home, the thought of writing a book and speaking for my career seemed very cool, but I didn't think I had the motivation to write one or work my way into the speaking business. However, right as I walked in my room when I got home, my heart and mind completely changed.

I then realized that God wanted me to write a book to share my story for the purpose of strengthening the faith of others, inspiring others, and possibly to open doors up to speak or coach.

Ironically, shortly after my talk with Missy, God showed me just how inspiring and impactful my story could be. One day while with my friends, Jonny Heidbrink and Emily Asche, at Emily's house, the topic of my story was brought up by Jonny while I was being introduced to Emily's parents. Earlier that day, I had shared my story with Jonny, which had a profound impact on his faith, so he figured it would have an impact on Emily's parents as well. After I finished telling them the story, they seemed stunned to hear about everything I had gone through. However, they were completely captivated when I told them my latest flashback about my experience in Heaven. After sharing my story with them, it only solidified my desire to share my story and the reason to why God had saved my life by the positive impact it had on Jonny, Emily, and Emily's parents.

*"Ben's story impacted and inspired me in more ways than one. It showed me how fragile life can be, but also reminded me how loving and merciful God is by miraculously saving his life. Overall though, it helped me refocus and ultimately strengthen my relationship with my Lord and Savior, Jesus Christ."* -Jonny Heidbrink

Everything seemed to be lining up perfectly in my life to the reason why God had saved my life, but I figured I should just pray about it and let things play out according to His will.

As I wrote during every spare moment throughout

the year, I would talk to God the whole time, because He would motivate me when I was tired and write through me when I was lost for words. This made our relationship even stronger, and it reminded me that with Him all things are possible, and even though we cannot see God, it doesn't mean He's not with us.

It seemed amazing to me to think about how much He had changed me in the past year. The year before, I never would have guessed that I would be writing a book or pursuing a career in speaking to glorify Him. However, He truly transformed my heart and mind to focus on Him, and strengthened me to help withstand the world's many temptations. I was then content with living the simple life and just staying in on the weekends by myself, which gave me the ultimate joy, because my happiness no longer relied on people's opinions of me, and I did not care about pleasing the world or trying to fit in anymore. I realized that true joy does not come from the world, but from God. And even if I lost everything, He would be enough.

### SUMMER 2013

Once I came home for the summer, I started working on the farm. Working on the farm was much more enjoyable than the previous summers because my Uncle Brian came home for the summer to help us, and I rarely get to see him, so having him home was a huge blessing. Every day we worked together we had Bible studies and in-depth conversations about God and the Bible. He opened my eyes to how important talking about and digging into your Bible every day is in strengthening your faith and relationship with God.

However, my farm work came to a stop when back pain

that I had been experiencing for months came to a breaking point. An MRI revealed degenerated disc disease and a herniated disc that was crushing my sciatic nerve in my right leg. The news was definitely not positive, considering I would not be able to work at the farm anymore or work at the Bible camp until my back was healthy. Camp started in a month, and this would be my last year counseling three of my senior high campers, Zach Feltman, Cole Rehovksy, and Zach Peterson, and could be my last year to counsel with my friends Dusek and Lindell. In addition, it was my cousin Isaiah's first year counseling. All this made the urge to regain my health much stronger.

Throughout June, I went to therapy twice a week and did more exercises at home, but nothing seemed to be helping. It was now time for camp to start and I was nowhere near healthy and the pain level was about the same as it was in May. Therefore, I had to tell my boss at camp that I was no longer able to counsel, since I could not run, jump, lift, or do any physical activity. I did not understand why this would happen now and became very frustrated, since I could not work at the bible camp and farm, or workout anymore.

One day as I was sitting at home, my mom and dad could see that I was down about my situation, and they reminded me to look at the positives that were coming out of this. One of them was that I would now have time to finish writing my story, because I had been so busy before that I was not able to write each day like I wanted to. It also gave me a chance to hang out with my friends, and I would have more time to train my players in the gym, even though I could not lift. When I thought about it, I knew they were right.

As I started to think positively about my situation,

things started to turn around for me. My back began to vastly improve and my pain levels went way down, to the point that I was able to counsel the senior high and junior high camps at the bible camp. And in the meantime, I was able to keep writing, catch up with old friends, and train my players in the gym. So I now look at it as a blessing, not heartbreak.

I have discovered throughout my journey that many of life's trials and disappointments are actually God's blessings in disguise. Through it all, He has strengthened me, taught me many life lessons, and blessed me with perseverance, which has enabled me to become the person I am today. His plan may not always make sense, but it is perfect, for He does not make mistakes.

Not only so, but we also glory in our sufferings, because we know that suffering produces perseverance; perseverance, character; and character, hope. And hope does not put us to shame, because God's love has been poured out into our hearts through the Holy Spirit, who has been given to us (Romans 5:3-5 NCV).

## Fall 2013

I am now in my senior year at the University of North Dakota, while pursuing a master's degree in counseling. Throughout the previous summer, my faith continued to grow, which has inspired me to start trying to live out each day solely for God and use the second chance He has given me to its full potential to honor and glorify Him. With that, it prompted me to start a weekly bible study in the attempt to help others strengthen their faith, and learn about and grow closer to the man who sacrificed himself on the cross for our sins, Jesus Christ, the Son of God. And with my friends, Lindell and Mayo, I was also inspired to soon establish something a little bigger and more complex than a weekly bible study, a Christian clothing company named, 'Purified.' In reality, starting a company seems impossible or foolish, since we are still in college and do not have the funds to start it yet, but after everything I have seen and learned throughout my journey so far; I know that with God, all things are possible.

I definitely have changed throughout the years, but I know the man I am becoming and striving to be is the person God wants and has wanted me to be all along. I do not know what my future holds, but I do know that no matter where He leads me in my life; He will be there to guide me and take care of me.

Now, looking back at it all, it seems miraculous to me that the tiny seed of faith that my parents had planted in me years before has grown and now blossomed through the power of God's love into something truly beautiful.

At first, April 6, 2007 was a day of great tragedy, but now, seven years later, it is a celebration of life and has become the ultimate blessing. That day has forever changed me, but only positively. It has brought me closer to my family than I ever imagined, proved to me that all things are possible with God and to never underestimate the power of prayer. It showed me that miracles still happen and God's love and forgiveness are immeasurable. Most of all, it gave me a strong relationship with God that will never be broken.

I now hope to keep sharing this story and the Word of God through my coaching and speaking to help people find new faith, inspire people who are already have faith, and to share His love not only through my words, but my actions. I want to thank God for all He has done for me and for sending His Son, Jesus Christ, to die on the cross, so we may be forgiven of our sins and have eternal life. Without Him, I would not be alive right now and for that, I am eternally grateful.

Jesus said, "Do not let your hearts be troubled. You believe in God; believe also in me. My Father's house has many rooms; if that were not so, would I have told you that I am going there to prepare a place for you? And if I go and prepare a place for you, I will come back and take you to be with me where I am" (John 14:1-3 NCV).

# Acknowledgements

**First and foremost,** I would like to thank God and His son, Jesus Christ, for blessing me with a second chance at life and giving me the opportunity to share my story. And also for helping me through the whole process by motivating me each day and writing through me when I was lost for words. Without them, this book would not have been possible.

My mom and dad: Thank you for always watching over me and reminding to put God first. And thanks also for all the unconditional love and support you have shown me throughout my life. God has truly blessed me with two amazing parents.

My sister, Christine: Thank you for always showing me what it is to be a strong person and for always being there when I need advice.

My brother, Andrew: Thank you for turning into the man of God that I could have only dreamed of being at your age. You are truly an inspiration to me by how hard you work each day while continuing to maintain a positive attitude through it all.

There are so many people who had a huge impact on my recovery and who supported my family and me that I could go on forever, so I want to thank everyone from the bottom of my heart for all the countless cards, letters, texts, e-mails, support, love, and prayers that everyone gave my family and me during that tough time. It was a huge part of what kept me going each day. Words cannot describe how much it meant to us and it will never be forgotten. Thank you, so much!

All the people who helped on the farm: My family and I give all of you a huge thank you because without you guys, we are not sure if the farm would have made it. Thanks again. All the help we received means more to us than you will ever know.

Altru Hospital Staff: Thank you for the excellent care you provided me through all the surgeries and the recovery that followed. And also for all the love and support I received from each of you every day. You guys were part of what motivated me to keep going every day, which meant the world to me.

My class of 2009: I cannot begin to explain how much all the support I received from you all meant to me. It was a time when I needed you guys the most, and you definitely did not disappoint. I was overjoyed with everything you did for my family and me, so thank you.

Mary Beth Lagerborg: Writing a book seemed very intimidating and I had many doubts at first, but God put you in my life to assist and guide me through it all. Thank you for giving me the confidence I needed in myself and for always being there if I needed anything. And also for all your patience, hard work, and care you have provided me. You are a friend and a true blessing to me.

Missy Ohe: Thank you for opening up my eyes to the idea of writing a book and for introducing me to the people that could make it possible. This whole process has positively changed me in more ways than one, so thank you for that also.

Mr. Beckman: Thank you for always being a good role model and great principal, but more importantly, a good friend.

Larry Biri: Thank you for generously taking the photos for my front and back covers, and also for allowing me to use the newspaper photos in my book that were photographed by you. It was greatly appreciated.

Uncle Brian, Uncle Daniel, and Uncle Robert: Thank you for helping me find the appropriate bible verses to use in my book and giving me many new ideas for my book along the way.

Joe Karas: Thank you for being an amazing physical trainer and motivating me every day to never give up. You are truly a genuine man.

Pastor Johnson: Thank you for postponing my class' confirmation date when I was in my accident, so I could be confirmed with them. That meant more to me than you will ever know.

Mr. Scherr: Thank for your kindness and guidance while giving me the opportunity to start my coaching career with you.

Beau Brunsvold: Thanks for always being a great family friend and always being there for me when I was down.

Austin Moe: Thank you for always staying positive and putting a smile on my face every time I see you. You are truly a brother to Andrew and me, and always will be.

Lin: Thank you for being one of the most kind-hearted people I know and for your friendship. Every time I see you, you inspire me by your strength and motivate me to be a better person. Love you, buddy.

# Photos

*Hylden family in 1999*

*Andrew and Ben carrying water to the calf barn 2006.*

*Ben with his grandfather, Duane Hylden, in 2001.*

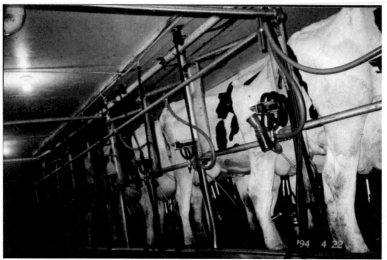

*Milking room*

*Bale shelter on south side of Hylden farm*

*Ben Hylden's sophomore picture. Photo by Kyle McFadden Photography.*
*Kylemcfadden.com. Used with permission.*

*Playing basketball sophomore year (before accident)*

*Andrew and Ben before first varsity game Ben's sophomore year*

*Ben's car after the accident April 6, 2007. Photo courtesy of Larry Biri, photographer. Photo appeared in the Walsh County Press, April 10, 2007.*

*Scene of accident. Photo courtesy of Larry Biri and Walsh County Press.*

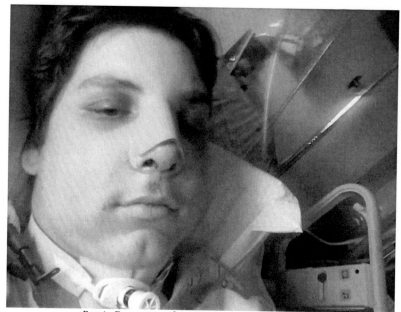

*Ben in Room 302, Altru Hospital, Grand Forks, ND*

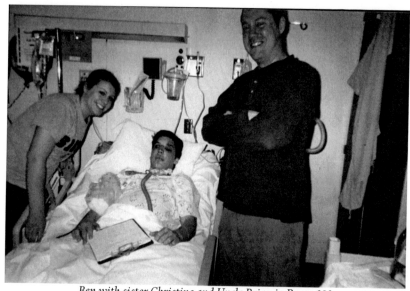

*Ben with sister Christine and Uncle Brian in Room 302*

*Chelsey Lutovsky and Ben right after he came out of the hospital*

*Lana, Ben, and Christine Hylden*

*On the farm after he came home from the hospital with Chelsey Lutovsky, Emily Mondry, and Amanda Barclay.*

*Top to bottom: Tyler Lindell, Ben, and Paul Dusek at Park River Bible Camp summer of 2012*

*Paul Dusek, Ben, and Tyler Lindell counseling at bible camp summer 2012.*

Cole Rehovsky, Ben, Zack Peterson, and Zach Feltman—three bible campers whom Ben has counseled every year he's worked at Park River Bible Camp, summer 2013.

Ben with younger brother Andrew at Andrew's junior prom in Park River, spring 2013.

*Ben with Evan Koenig at a choir concert, spring of 2010*

*Paul Dusek and Ben at their senior prom*
*in Grafton, spring 2010*

*Ben's high school graduation. Photo courtesy of Larry Biri and the Walsh County Press.*

*Hylden family at the wedding of Christine to Jared Ohma 2013*

*Photo courtesy of Larry Biri.*